WHAT BIRD IS THIS ?

HENRY HILL COLLINS, JR.

Illustrated by

Russell Francis Peterson

DOVER PUBLICATIONS, INC.

NEW YORK

Published in Canada by General Publishing Company, Ltd., 30 Lesmill Road, Don Mills, Toronto, Ontario.

Published in the United Kingdom by Constable and Company Ltd., 10 Orange Street, London W. C. 2.

This Dover edition, first published in 1965, is an unabridged and unaltered republication of the work originally published by Harper & Brothers, Publishers, New York, in 1961 under the title *The Bird Watcher's Quiz Book*. This edition is published by special arrangement with Harper & Brothers.

International Standard Book Number: 0-486-21490-7
Library of Congress Catalog Card Number: 65-27017

Manufactured in the United States of America

Dover Publications, Inc.
180 Varick Street
New York, N. Y. 10014

CONTENTS

FOR THE EXPERT

FOR THE SPECIALIST

INTRODUCTION

The first bird quiz I ever tried was on a field trip to Cape May, New Jersey, with the Delaware Valley Ornithological Club on a Memorial Day excursion many years ago. Not much constructive birding could be done from the train window of the West Jersey and Seashore's *Fishermen's Special*. Some of us, therefore, used the ride to quiz one another on field marks, colors, and habits of various species, particularly those we might see that day at the shore.

In later years, automobile trips from New York to Cape Ann, Cape Cod, or to Orient, Long Island, have been the occasion for more elaborate quizzes, many of them also dealing with field identification. The fun that all of us had who participated in these games and the conviction that quizzes were an easy way to learn solid facts about birds led to the writing of this book.

The four divisions of the book—for the Amateur, Advanced, Expert, and Specialist—are quite general. The specialist in one field of bird watching may be of only amateur standing in another. The expert on the birds of one region may be a novice somewhere else. You may find some quizzes for the expert easier than certain ones in the advanced section. Some players may be baffled by one amateur quiz, and yet do well on questions in other sections. Try them all. You may find that some of those in the expert or specialist section are not so hard as they may look at first glance.

As travel becomes easier, bird watchers are becoming increasingly interested in species in different parts of the country. Many persons go south to see new birds in winter, west or east to see them in summer, and they are always on the lookout for rarities at their home feeders in the colder months. A number of quizzes, therefore, include some birds outside your region.

Most questions involve species that occur annually both east and west of the Rocky Mountains. However, if the correct answer to a question depends upon knowledge of a species or subspecies that occurs annually only east of the Rockies or only from the Rockies west, that question is marked (E) or (W) accordingly. ("Rockies" as a line of demarcation means "Yukon Territory, Rocky Mountains, and Pecos Valley." The Black Hills and the Lower Rio Grande Valley are east of the Rockies.) If there are a number of questions marked (E) or (W) they are usually placed at the end of a quiz. Eastern or western quiz-takers can then readily omit either of these, if they wish, and adjust their score accordingly.

Series of bird names within quizzes are generally listed in alphabetical rather than taxonomic order. Species names, unless otherwise stated, are those of the American Ornithologists' Union (A. O. U.), *Check-list of North American Birds*, fifth edition, 1957. Each quiz is designed to cover broadly the subject of its title, not to bolster the ego of the player. In consequence, many a good birder may find that 50 per cent is a good score. On certain of the tougher quizzes, it may be more fun to give yourself a handicap. For example, count each correct answer 7 or 8 instead of 5.

Many of the quizzes bring out key points in field identification.

INTRODUCTION

A serious student will find them a pleasant way to increase his knowledge. Any person who learns all the answers to all the quizzes will have a solid foundation—and quite a superstructure—of facts about birds and bird watching.

Take this book with you on field trips. Use it alone or make a game of the quizzes with your companions. Quiz the other people in the car or train on the way to your destination. Play the quizzes as a game at the diner or in your motel room; or when stretched out on a sunny dune after lunch; or when huddled in a mountainside cabin waiting for the rain to stop. Some questions you may find easy, perhaps too easy. But if the answers to others elude you, remember that they might well have eluded Audubon and Wilson also.

H. H. C. Jr.

Scarsdale, New York
April 15, 1961

FOR THE AMATEUR

Shoveler Baldpate Pintail Black Duck Mallard Gadwall

POND DUCKS DABBLING

1. FIRST BIRD WALK

Fill in the blanks from the list of 20 common birds below.

An old-timer took me on my first bird walk one spring morning. A House_____(1) flew up as we started down the path. On the lawn a short-tailed, shiny black_____(2) waddled about near where a _____(3) was standing, head cocked listening for worms.

A crested_____(4) shrieked in the oak tree up which a Downy _____(5) was hitching its way. In contrast a Brown_____(6) spiraled up the neighboring tree where our_____(7) Owl was looking out of its hole. Overhead a_____(8) cawed and a_____(9) was flying from the bay or lake to its favorite garbage dump. From a thicket came the vigorous scratching of a_____(10) and from a branch above it we saw, and heard the unoiled squeak of, the Brown-headed_____(11). Nearby on the feeder a Black-capped_____(12), a White-breasted_____(13), and a Redwinged_____(14) were busy eating.

Over the garden a black and yellow_____(15) bounced in characteristic flight. An orange and black_____(16) piped its treetop welcome to spring in loud whistles. From the barn door a fork-tailed_____(17) whizzed out. On a dead apple tree perched that harbinger of spring, the_____(18).

From the distant creek came the rattle of a_____(19) flying to its lookout perch over the water. Near at hand from a maple I heard the dry trill of the Chipping_____(20).

My first half-hour in the field that spring taught me how easy it was to see 20 species of birds.

20 Common Birds

a. American Goldfinch
b. Barn Swallow
c. Blackbird
d. Belted Kingfisher
e. Bluebird (Eastern or Western)
f. Chickadee
g. Creeper
h. Cowbird
i. Crow (Common, Fish, or Northwestern)
j. Finch, Sparrow, or Wren
k. Gull (California, Herring, or other species)
l. Jay (Blue or Steller's)
m. Nuthatch
n. Oriole (Baltimore or Bullock's)
o. Robin
p. Screech
q. Sparrow
r. Starling
s. Towhee (Rufous-sided, Abert's, or Brown)
t. Woodpecker

2. BIRD NAMES—COLOR

Amateurs page through their bird guides many times as they look up new birds. Often they stop to browse and read about species from different parts of the country. Soon such people learn the names of many species that they have not yet seen and that they may not see for some time. But in this way, through names at least, they become acquainted with the wealth of North American bird life. Quizzes 2, 3, and 4 are designed to test the results of such browsing. Each species occurs annually somewhere in North America. Fill in the blanks to make a correct species name of a North American bird. Each correct answer counts 4.

1. Black_____
2. Blue_____
3. Blue-gray_____
4. Brown_____
5. Cinnamon_____
6. Glaucous_____
7. Golden_____
8. Gray_____
9. Great Blue_____
10. Great Gray_____
11. Great White (E)____
12. Green_____

13. Indigo (E)_____
14. Ivory_____
15. Lazuli_____
16. Purple_____
17. Red_____
18. Ruddy_____
19. Rusty_____
20. Scarlet (E)_____
21. Snow_____
22. Snowy_____
23. Sooty_____
24. White_____

25. Yellow_____

SLATE-COLORED JUNCO

2

3. BIRD NAMES—RED, WHITE, AND BLACK

Fill in the blanks to make a correct species name for a North American bird. Each correct answer counts 4.

1. Red-bellied (E)_____
2. Red-necked_____
3. Red-shafted_____
4. Red-shouldered_____
5. Red-tailed_____
6. Redwinged_____
7. White-breasted_____
8. White-crowned_____
9. White-eyed (E)_____
10. White-fronted_____
11. White-tailed_____
12. White-throated_____

13. White-winged_____
14. Black-and-white (E)_____
15. Black-backed_____
16. Black-bellied_____
17. Black-billed_____
18. Black-capped_____
19. Black-crowned_____
20. Black-headed_____
21. Black-necked_____
22. Blackpoll_____
23. Black-throated Blue (E)_____
24. Black-throated Gray (W)_____

25. Black-throated Green (E)_____

RED-BREASTED MERGANSER

4.   BIRD NAMES—HABITAT

The common names of many birds often refer to characteristic habitats. Fill in the blanks to make a correct name of a species of North American bird. Each correct answer counts 4.

1. Bank_____

2. Barn_____

3. Cedar_____

4. Cliff_____

5. House_____

6. Marsh_____

7. Mountain_____

8. Myrtle_____

9. Rock_____

10. Sage_____

11. Sandhill_____

12. Savannah_____

13. Snow_____

14. Spruce._____

15. Surf_____

16. Tree_____

17. Upland_____

18. Water_____

19. Wood_____

East only

20. Field_____

21. Magnolia_____

22. Orchard_____

23. Palm_____

24. Pine_____

25. Prairie_____

TREE SPARROW

4

5. SIZE AND MESSMATES

Size is important in learning to identify birds. The standard scale is: Sparrow, 6 inches; Robin, 10 inches; Pigeon, 15 inches; Crow, 20 inches. Food habits are important, too. Insect-eating birds have thin bills, seed-eating birds have heavy, thick bills. Those of meat-eaters are usually hooked, those of fish-eaters may have saw-toothed edges. Each fully correct answer counts 10; partially correct answers count proportionally.

Size

1. Arrange these species in order of size, smallest to largest: Common Crow, Yellow-billed Cuckoo, Ruby-throated or Anna's Hummingbird, Rock Dove, Robin, Downy Woodpecker.

2. Arrange these species in order of size, largest to smallest: Great Crested Flycatcher (E), Boat-tailed Grackle, Blue or Steller's Jay, Horned Lark, Tree Swallow, House Wren.

3. Pick out the four species that are about the same size: Catbird, Golden-crowned Kinglet, Mockingbird, Ovenbird, Hermit Thrush, Tufted Titmouse, House Sparrow, Red-eyed Vireo.

4. Put these species into three groupings, each with birds of approximately the same size: Brown-headed Cowbird, Sparrow Hawk, Killdeer, Baltimore or Bullock's Oriole, American Redstart, Chipping Sparrow, Starling, Yellow Warbler, Whip-poor-will.

5. From this list pick out the four birds that are about the same size: Bobwhite, Mourning Dove, Red-shafted or Yellow-shafted Flicker, Belted Kingfisher, Barn Owl, Chimney or Vaux's Swift, Brown Thrasher (E).

Food Habits

Pick out from the lists in each question three species with similar food preferences.

6. Wood Duck, Bald Eagle, Herring Gull, Common Loon, Common Snipe, Turkey Vulture.

7. Blue-gray Gnatcatcher, Pied-billed Grebe, Pintail, Veery, Red-eyed Vireo, Greater Yellowlegs.

8. Bobwhite, Canvasback, American Goldfinch, Green Heron, Least Sandpiper, White-throated Sparrow.

9. Peregrine Falcon, Canada Goose, Ruffed Grouse, Cooper's Hawk, Screech Owl, Red-breasted Merganser.

10. Red-tailed Hawk, Great Blue Heron, Killdeer, Belted Kingfisher, Mallard, Common Tern.

6. IDENTIFICATION BY COLOR

Some birds common over much of North America in summer have striking and distinct colors (notably the males) and are easy to learn and to remember. Some of the easiest are given below. Match the description with the species. Each correct answer counts 5.

Species

Black conspicuous

1. Brown-headed Cowbird, male ☐
2. Crow (Common, Fish, or Northwestern) ☐
3. Oriole (Baltimore or Bullock's), male ☐
4. Redwinged Blackbird, male ☐
5. Starling ☐

Blue or blue-gray conspicuous

6. Belted Kingfisher ☐
7. Bluebird (Eastern or Western) ☐
8. Great Blue Heron ☐

Gray conspicuous

9. Black-capped Chickadee ☐
10. Junco (Oregon, Slate-colored, or other) ☐
11. Mockingbird ☐
12. Titmouse (Plain or Tufted) ☐
13. White-breasted Nuthatch ☐

Red conspicuous

14. Cardinal, male ☐
15. Robin ☐
16. Scarlet Tanager, male (E) ☐
17. Summer Tanager, male ☐

Yellow conspicuous

18. American Goldfinch ☐
19. Yellowthroat ☐
20. Yellow Warbler ☐

Description

a. All black
b. All red, no crest
c. All red with a crest
d. Almost all yellow
e. Black and orange
f. Black with a brown head
g. Black with red shoulders
h. Blue and white with a crest, short tail
i. Blue with a red breast
j. Gray above and on breast, white outer tail-feathers
k. Gray above, black crown, white cheeks and underparts, stubby
l. Gray above with a black cap and bib
m. Gray with a crest
n. Gray with white on wings, long tail
o. Long neck, long legs, sharp bill; blue-gray
p. Brick-red breast, dark back
q. Red with black wings and tail
r. Shiny black with little dots, short tail
s. Olive above, yellow below, with a black mask
t. Yellow with black cap, wings, and tail

7. CHARACTERISTIC HABITATS

Each species of bird has its preferred home area or habitat. Some species occur in several. Others are found in only one or in a very limited number. Many species have a *characteristic habitat* with which we customarily identify them. Match the characteristic habitat below with the appropriate species by placing the right letter in the box. Each correct answer counts 5.

Species	Characteristic Habitat
1. American Bittern ☐	a. Airport
2. Bluebird (Eastern or Western) ☐	b. Apple trees and streamside shrubbery
3. Bobolink ☐	c. City streets
4. Clapper Rail ☐	d. Deep woods
5. Common Loon ☐	e. Dry hillsides and bushy fields
6. Field Sparrow ☐	
7. Great Horned Owl ☐	f. Dry woods
8. Horned Lark ☐	g. Field
9. House Sparrow ☐	h. Forest floor
10. House Wren ☐	i. Fresh-water marsh
11. Meadowlark (Eastern or Western) ☐	j. Kitchen garden
	k. Meadow
12. Mockingbird ☐	l. Moist woods
13. Ovenbird ☐	m. Northern lake
14. Pied-billed Grebe ☐	n. Orchard
15. Rufous-sided Towhee ☐	o. Pond with reeds and lily pads
16. Scarlet Tanager (E) ☐	
17. Veery ☐	p. Salt marsh
18. White-eyed Vireo ☐	q. Shade trees
19. Wood Thrush (E) ☐	r. Southern garden
20. Yellow Warbler ☐	s. Thicket
	t. Upper canopy of trees

8. IDENTIFICATION BY HABITS

Many common species of birds have characteristic and conspicuous habits. Match the species with the habit by placing the right letter in the box. Each correct answer counts 5.

Habit

1. Catches fish in its talons ☐
2. Climbs down trunk of tree head first ☐
3. Climbs straight up tree trunk ☐
4. Dives at head of intruder into nesting area ☐
5. Dives for fish from streamside perch or midair ☐
6. Flies up to attack passing hawk or crow ☐
7. Flushes from roadside gravel with audible whir ☐
8. Flushes with explosive sound from upland woods ☐
9. Patrols lawn in hops and short runs ☐
10. Perches hunched-up on roadside wire ☐
11. Runs back and forth at edge of waves ☐
12. Scratches with both feet at once in thicket ☐
13. Sings through heat of day from wire or twig ☐
14. Sings through heat of day in tree ☐
15. Soars high in sky, often in circles ☐
16. Spirals up tree trunk ☐
17. Stands upright motionless in marsh ☐
18. Teeters as it patrols shoreline of pond or stream ☐
19. Waddles on green ☐
20. Walks on ground (long, black tail) ☐

Species

a. Belted Kingfisher
b. Brown Creeper
c. Common Grackle
d. Common Tern
e. Downy Woodpecker
f. Eastern Bluebird
g. Eastern Kingbird, Redwinged Blackbird
h. Fox Sparrow
i. Great Blue Heron
j. Indigo Bunting (E)
k. Mourning Dove
l. Osprey
m. Red-eyed Vireo
n. Robin
o. Ruffed Grouse
p. Sanderling
q. Solitary Sandpiper, Spotted Sandpiper
r. Starling
s. Turkey Vulture
t. White-breasted Nuthatch

9. IDENTIFICATION ON GROUND OR PERCH

Certain families or groups of birds have characteristic attitudes or behavior on the ground or perch. Knowing these habits is a big help in narrowing down the field of possibilities for a strange bird and trying to identify it as to species. In this quiz, match the family or group with the description by putting in the box the right letter. Each correct answer counts 5.

Description	Family or Group
1. Appear to walk under water ☐	a. Auks, Murres
2. Cling head down to trunk of tree ☐	b. Creepers
3. Cling to bark of tree, supported by tail, and advance upward head first and with a series of jerks ☐	c. Dippers
4. Cling to bark of tree, supported by tail, and spiral upward around trunk ☐	d. Goatsuckers (Nighthawks, Whip-poor-will)
5. Eyes, when on road shoulder, often gleam in headlights ☐	e. Gulls
6. Feign broken wing to lure intruders from nest ☐	f. Hawks
7. Follow a farmer plowing to feed on insects, etc., turned up by plow ☐	g. Herons
8. Have start-and-stop manner of feeding on a mud flat ☐	h. Horned Larks, Pipits
9. Land straddle-legged, stand or sit upright, and walk poorly ☐	i. Hummingbirds
10. Like large, open spaces; walk and run, do not hop; inconspicuous when motionless ☐	j. Jays
11. Many members of group sing (often persistently) from weedtop or bushtop ☐	k. Nuthatches
12. Move fairly continuously when feeding on a mud flat ☐	l. Owls
13. Often have favorite observation post with wide view ☐	m. Plovers
14. Often hop up a tree from branch to branch in a spiral around the trunk ☐	n. Sandpipers
15. Perch on tiny twigs or on man-made wires ☐	o. Shorebirds
16. Perch upright; with seeming convulsions occasionally regurgitate pellets of indigestible food ☐	p. Sparrows
17. Roost vertically, clinging to crevices in cliffs or to inside of chimneys or hollow trees ☐	q. Surface-feeding Ducks
18. Several species often perch together on a telegraph wire ☐	r. Swallows
19. Stand motionless for hours in shallow water waiting to catch a fish ☐	s. Swifts
20. Waddle, rather than walk, on land ☐	t. Woodpeckers

10. IDENTIFICATION BY FLIGHT—
FAMILIES OR GROUPS

Certain families or groups of birds have a characteristic flight. Being able to recognize this is a great help in narrowing down the field of possibilities for a strange bird and trying to identify it as to species. In this quiz, match the family or group with the flight description by putting in the box the right letter. Each correct answer counts 5.

Description	Family or Group
1. Can fly backward ☐	a. Accipiters
2. Dive vertically into the water for bait fish ☐	b. Alcids
3. Flit close to the surface of the sea, as if walking on water ☐	c. Buteos
4. Flocks often fly compactly and wheel in unison ☐	d. Cranes
5. Fly on ultra-silent wings ☐	e. Diving Ducks
6. Have swift, buzzy, veering flight ☐	f. Falcons
7. Hawks with broad, fingered wings and fan-shaped tails ☐	g. Flycatchers
8. Hawks with long, pointed wings ☐	h. Geese
9. Hawks with short, rounded wings and long tails ☐	i. Gulls
10. Long-legged, long-necked birds that fly with legs extended but necks drawn in ☐	j. Herons
11. Long-legged, long-necked birds that fly with neck and legs fully extended ☐	k. Hummingbirds
12. Most have gently undulating flight ☐	l. Owls
13. Noted for their swift, graceful flight ☐	m. Petrels
14. Often fly high and in wedges ☐	n. Rails
15. Often follow ships, soaring over the stern ☐	o. Shearwaters
16. Perch on dead limbs from which they sally out to catch insects ☐	p. Shorebirds
17. Sail close to the surface of the waves on set wings	q. Surface-feeding Ducks
18. Take off by first pattering along the surface of the water ☐	r. Swallows
19. Take off from water by jumping directly in the air ☐	s. Terns
20. Usually dangle their legs on their weak flights ☐	t. Woodpeckers

11. IDENTIFICATION BY FLIGHT—SPECIES

The flight of some species is quite characteristic and by it a bird can often be recognized at a great distance. Check the appropriate box for the species that fits the flight description. Each correct answer counts 5.

Description	Species
1. A dark duck; in flight, wings show silver lining	☐ Black Duck (E) ☐ Scoter
2. Black, stubby; short, triangular wings; flocks perform intricate revolutions in the air	☐ Redwinged Blackbird, ☐ Starling
3. Flight level; red breast, white rear flanks	☐ Bluebird ☐ Robin
4. Large, black; flies with strong flaps, soars with wings in shallow V	☐ Crow ☐ Raven
5. Large, black; long wings and tail; soars on V-shaped wings, seldom flaps	☐ Bald Eagle ☐ Turkey Vulture
6. Large; neck drawn in, legs trailing	☐ Great Blue Heron ☐ Sandhill Crane
7. Large; long, black neck; flies high in V-shaped wedge	☐ Brant (E) ☐ Canada Goose
8. Large, white; neck drawn in, legs trailing	☐ Common Egret ☐ Herring Gull
9. Long, curved, pointed wings; very erratic flight, usually high in air	☐ Common Snipe ☐ Nighthawk
10. Long, forked tail; swift, graceful flight	☐ Barn Swallow ☐ Cliff Swallow
11. Low, undulating flight with bird showing a white rump	☐ Flicker ☐ Yellowlegs
12. Long, pointed wings, long tail, flight swift, sometimes hovers	☐ Mourning Dove ☐ Sparrow Hawk
13. Male (except first year) all dark, female light below; graceful, swift, masterful flight	☐ Purple Martin ☐ Tree Swallow
14. Medium sized, black; keel-shaped tail, flight horizontal	☐ Cowbird ☐ Grackle
15. Roller-coaster flight	☐ Goldfinch ☐ Warbler
16. Similar to (5) but tail very short; flaps more	☐ Black Vulture ☐ Red-tailed Hawk
17. Small, looks like a flying cigar; wings flicker, flight erratic, often high in air	☐ Hummingbird ☐ Swift
18. Very large, dark; near water; soars on horizontal wings	☐ Bald Eagle ☐ Cormorant
19. White, soars or flies back and forth, often over lake or coastal city	☐ Common Tern ☐ Herring Gull
20. Wings fingered, flight horizontal; birds cross open space one at a time	☐ Blue or Steller's Jay ☐ Mourning Dove

12. FOR THE BIRD LISTENER

Knowing a bird's call or song is one of the easiest ways to identify it. Some birds have highly distinctive voices. Certain songs and calls by onomatopoeia have given rise to bird names. Here are some of the best known. Match the species with the description of its voice by putting in the box the key letter of the species. Each correct answer counts 5.

Description	Species
1. A brusque *FEE-bee* ☐	a. Black-capped Chickadee
2. A carol, *cheerily cheer up, cheerily cheer up* ☐	b. Blue Jay (E)
3. A catlike *mew* ☐	c. Bobolink
4. A clear whistled *poor BOB WHITE* ☐	d. Bobwhite
5. A crisp, clear *peet-weet* from low over the water ☐	e. Cardinal
6. A distinctive, easy-to-learn, but variable *which IS it, which IS it, which IS it?* ☐	f. Catbird
7. A dry, pleasing *drink your TEA-E-E-E* or *drink YOUR tea-e-e-e* ☐	g. Common Crow
8. A loud, clear whistle, *wheat, wheat, wheat, what-cheer, what-cheer, what-cheer* ☐	h. Eastern Goldfinch
9. A loud cry, *KillDEEER* ☐	i. Eastern Phoebe
10. A loud ringing *teaCHER, tea-CHER, teaCHER*, more accurately, *you're rich, You're Rich, YOU'RE RICH* ☐	j. Eastern Wood Pewee
11. A nasal *yank, yank, yank* ☐	k. Killdeer
12. A noisy shriek, *jay, jay* ☐	l. Ovenbird
13. A pleasing *oo-long TEA* ☐	m. Redwing Blackbird
14. A rich, bubbling *bob-o-link, bob-o-link, spink, spank, spink* ☐	n. Robin
15. A set of clear whistles, *Old SAM PEAbody, PEAbody, PEAbody* ☐	o. Rufous-sided Towhee
16. A sweet, plaintive *PEE-week, PEE-a-WEE* ☐	p. Spotted Sandpiper
17. Call, a *chick-a-dee-dee-dee* ☐	q. White-breasted Nuthatch
18. *Caw, Caw* ☐	r. White-throated Sparrow
19. *Per-CHICK-o-ree*, from top of rise in bounding flight ☐	s. Yellowthroat
20. *Sweet, sweet, sweet, I'm so sweet* (from the May garden, orchard, or streamside shrubbery) ☐	t. Yellow Warbler

13. IDENTIFICATION BY RANGE AND SEASON

All birds have certain geographic areas—called ranges—in which they live at certain seasons of the year. In learning to identify birds, it helps to know if the bird is supposed to be in that general area at that season of the year. Test your knowledge of birds' ranges by putting the correct code letter A, B, C, D, or E in the box after the names of the species in the list below. Each correct answer counts 5.

A - Not usually seen in the United States in winter (if seen, only in Florida).
B - East of the Rockies only.
C - West of the Rockies only.
D - South of New Hampshire only.
E - Florida only.

Species

1. American Woodcock ☐
2. Blue Jay ☐
3. Bobolink ☐
4. Broad-winged Hawk ☐
5. Brown Thrasher ☐
6. California Quail ☐
7. Cardinal ☐
8. Common Bushtit
9. Common Grackle ☐
10. Everglade Kite ☐
11. Flamingo ☐
12. Great White Heron ☐
13. Osprey ☐
14. Purple Martin ☐
15. Red-legged Kittiwake ☐
16. Rose-breasted Grosbeak ☐
17. Scarlet Tanager ☐
18. Tufted Titmouse ☐
19. Varied Thrush ☐
20. Carolina Chickadee ☐

GREEN HERON

WHOOPING CRANE

SANDHILL CRANE

14. CONSERVATION

Check the appropriate box or boxes, or fill in the correct word.
Each correct answer counts 5.

1. Agricultural development and insufficient protection threaten certain of our shorebirds that winter in ☐ Argentina ☐ Brazil ☐ Chile.
2. After complete protection for over 40 years, which of these birds has shown a particularly conspicuous comeback? ☐ Warblers ☐ Shorebirds ☐ Sparrows ☐ Thrushes
3. A Sharp-shinned Hawk catches a chickadee. Is that ☐ good ☐ bad ☐ neither?
4. Conservationists in general feel that the greatest threat to most wildlife today is from ☐ loss of habitat ☐ too much hunting.
5. Destruction of the primeval forest of the South has spelled the doom of the_____.
6. Inbreeding, disease, and brush fires in their last refuge, on the island of Martha's Vineyard, were responsible for the extermination of the_____ in 1931.
7. In the stomach of one Brewer's Blackbird, biologists found the remains of ☐ 42 ☐ 442 ☐ 4442 ☐ 44,442 injurious alfalfa weevils.
8. Market hunting and destruction of the great oak and beech forests was responsible for the extermination of the_____.
9. Market hunting of old on the prairies in spring and in Canada in fall, and continued inadequate protection in Patagonia in winter have almost finished the_____.
10. Owls are regarded as particularly valuable to agriculture because of the vast numbers of ☐ night-flying insects ☐ rodents that they eat.
11. What once-greatly-threatened shorebird whose population has still not reached its former abundance has a range that is shown on the map below?

14. CONSERVATION *(Continued)*

12. The Great Auk was exterminated by 1844 because of ☐ a long series of unfavorable seasons for breeding ☐ excessive commercial exploitation ☐ volcanic disturbances that destroyed its main breeding islands.

13. The most serious new threat to wildlife seems to be ☐ atomic radiation ☐ excessive use of powerful pesticides.

14. The National Association of Audubon Societies was formed in 1895 primarily because of excessive ☐ demand for songbirds for gourmets' meals ☐ robbing of birds' nests by collectors ☐ slaughter of egrets for their plumes for women's hats.

15. The Santa Ynez National Forest is the last refuge of the ☐ Aplomado Falcon ☐ California Condor ☐ White-tailed Kite.

16. The National Wildlife Refuges, which provide sanctuary for millions of waterfowl, also have a human visitation each year of some ☐ 2,000,000 ☐ 8,000,000 ☐ 16,000,000 persons.

17. The world's first sanctuary for hawks is at_____.

18. Studies by Government biologists have shown that virtually the only hawks that ever take chickens are ☐ bird hawks (accipiters) ☐ falcons ☐ soaring hawks (buteos), and that these do not take any appreciable number.

19. Which of these habitats are conservationists today most concerned about preserving? ☐ deserts ☐ mountaintops ☐ wetlands

20. Which of these habitats is more threatened today? ☐ barrier beaches ☐ virgin prairie

HUDSONIAN GODWIT

AMERICAN WOODCOCK

15. POPULAR NAMES

Match the official *A.O.U. Check-list* name with the local or vernacular name by placing the correct key letter in the box. Each correct answer counts 5.

A. O. U. Check-list Name

1. American Goldfinch ☐
2. Anhinga ☐
3. Common Nighthawk ☐
4. Common Tern ☐
5. Barn Owl ☐
6. Eskimo Curlew
7. Gray Jay ☐
8. Green Heron ☐
9. Pileated Woodpecker ☐
10. Rock Dove ☐
11. Scaup ☐
12. Semipalmated Sandpiper ☐
13. White-throated Sparrow ☐
14. Yellow-shafted Flicker ☐

East only

15. Baltimore Oriole ☐
16. Black-billed Cuckoo ☐
17. Common Grackle ☐
18. Least Flycatcher ☐
19. Ovenbird ☐
20. Sooty Tern ☐

Local or Vernacular Name

a. Bluebill
b. Bullbat
c. Chebec
d. Common Pigeon
e. Crow Blackbird
f. Doughbird
g. Fly-up-the-creek
h. Hang-nest
i. High-hole
j. Log Cock
k. Monkey-faced Owl
l. Peabody bird
m. Peep
n. Rain Crow
o. Sea Swallow
p. Snakebird
q. Teacherbird
r. Whiskey Jack
s. Wideawake
t. Wild Canary

FOR THE ADVANCED

DOUBLE-CRESTED CORMORANT

16. GUNNERS' NAMES

Hunters often have different names for game birds from those used by bird watchers. Match the *A.O.U. Check-list* names with these gunners' names by placing the correct key letter in the box. Each correct answer counts 5.

Gunners' Name	A.O.U. Check-list Name
1. Baldpate ☐	a. American Coot
2. Bluebill ☐	b. American Widgeon
3. Blue Peter ☐	c. American Woodcock
4. Blue Wavy (E) ☐	d. Blue Goose
5. Broadbill ☐	e. Bufflehead
6. Butterball ☐	f. Canada Goose
7. Can ☐	g. Canvasback
8. Greenhead ☐	h. Common Goldeneye
9. Honker ☐	i. Gray Partridge
10. Hun ☐	j. Mallard
11. Little Wavy ☐	k. Pintail
12. Partridge ☐	l. Ross' Goose
13. Sea Coot ☐	m. Ruddy Duck
14. Specklebelly ☐	n. Ruffed Grouse
15. Spiketail ☐	o. Scaup
16. Spoonbill ☐	p. Scaup
17. Sprig ☐	q. Scoter
18. Timberdoodle (E) ☐	r. Shoveler
19. Whistler ☐	s. Snow Goose
20. White Wavy ☐	t. White-fronted Goose

Adult   Immature

BLUE GOOSE

17. COLOR-PATTERN NAMES

Test your knowledge of species in the *A.O.U. Check-list* (no accidentals). Fill in each blank to make a correct species name for a North American bird. Each correct answer counts 2 1/2.

1. Buff-breasted _____
2. Chestnut-collared _____
3. Golden-crowned _____
4. Golden-fronted _____
5. Gray-cheeked _____
6. Green-winged _____
7. Green-tailed _____
8. Olive-backed _____
9. Olive-sided _____
10. Orange-crowned _____
11. Ruby-crowned _____
12. Rufous-crowned _____
13. White-winged (range map at lower left) _____
14. White-winged (range map at lower right) _____
15. Yellow-billed _____
16. Yellow-breasted _____
17. Yellow-headed _____
18. Yellow-shafted _____

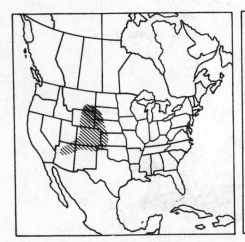
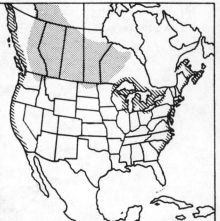

17. COLOR-PATTERN NAMES *(Continued)*

East only

19. Bay-breasted _____
20. Blue-winged _____
21. Brown-headed _____
22. Buff-bellied _____
23. Chestnut-sided _____
24. Golden-cheeked _____
25. Golden-winged _____
26. Ivory-billed _____
27. Rose-breasted _____
28. Rose-throated _____
29. Ruby-throated _____
30. Yellow-throated _____

West only

31. Ash-throated _____
32. Blue-throated _____
33. Chestnut-backed _____
34. Coppery-tailed _____
35. Glaucous-winged _____
36. Gray-headed _____
37. Pink-footed _____
38. Rufous-necked _____
39. Rufous-winged _____
40. Sulphur-bellied _____

RED-NECKED GREBE

18. PATTERN AND STRUCTURE NAMES

Test your knowledge of species in the *A.O.U. Check-list* (no accidentals). Fill in each blank to make a correct species name for a North American bird. Each correct answer counts 2 1/2.

Pattern

1. Belted _____
2. Hooded _____
3. Ladder-backed _____
4. Marbled _____
5. Pectoral _____
6. Pied-billed _____
7. Ring-billed _____
8. Ring-necked _____
9. Ringed _____
10. Scaled _____
11. Zone-tailed _____

East only

12. Barred _____
13. Mottled _____
14. Spotted-breasted _____

West only

15. Band-tailed _____
16. Bar-tailed _____
17. Bridled _____
18. Plain _____
19. Spectacled _____
20. Spotted _____

18. PATTERN AND STRUCTURE NAMES *(Continued)*

Structure

21. Broad-tailed _____

22. Curve-billed _____

23. Gull-billed _____

24. Long-billed _____

25. Long-eared _____

26. Long-tailed _____

27. Rough-legged _____

28. Rough-winged _____

29. Scissor-tailed _____

30. Sharp-shinned _____

31. Sharp-tailed _____

32. Short-eared _____

East only

33. Broad-winged _____

34. Short-billed _____

35. Short-tailed _____

36. Swallow-tailed _____

West only

37. Broad-billed _____

38. Bristle-thighed _____

39. Slender-billed _____

40. Thick-billed _____

LOGGERHEAD SHRIKE

19. PLACE NAMES

Test your knowledge of species in the *A.O.U. Check-list*. Fill in each blank to make a correct species name of a North American bird. Each correct answer counts 2 1/2.

1. American _____

2. Arctic _____

3. Bohemian _____

4. Canada _____

5. Caspian _____

6. European _____

7. Lapland _____

8. Manx _____

9. Nashville _____

10. Oregon _____

11. Tennessee _____

12. Virginia _____

East only

13. Acadian _____

14. Bahamas _____

15. Baltimore _____

16. Bermuda _____

17. Cape May _____

18. Cape Sable _____

19. Carolina _____

20. Colima _____

AMERICAN CROW

24

19. PLACE NAMES *(Continued)*

21. Connecticut _____
22. Eurasian _____
23. Hudsonian _____
24. Iceland _____
25. Ipswich _____
26. Kentucky _____
27. Labrador _____
28. Louisiana _____
29. Mississippi _____
30. Philadelphia _____
31. South Trinidad _____
32. West Indian _____

West only

33. Aleutian _____
34. Arizona _____
35. California _____
36. Gila _____
37. Guadalupe _____
38. Laysan _____
39. Mexican _____
40. New Zealand _____

OREGON JUNCO

20. BIRD GEOGRAPHY

Match the bird and the geographic location with which it is often associated by placing the correct key letter in the box. Each correct answer counts 5.

1. Bicknell's Thrush ☐
2. Colima Warbler ☐
3. Dusky Seaside Sparrow ☐
4. Everglade Kite ☐
5. Golden-cheeked Warbler ☐
6. Great Auk ☐
7. Greater Snow Goose ☐
8. Great White Heron ☐
9. Heath Hen ☐
10. Ipswich Sparrow ☐
11. Ivory-billed Woodpecker ☐
12. Kirtland's Warbler ☐
13. Leach's Petrel ☐
14. Sooty Tern ☐
15. Trumpeter Swan ☐
16. Whistling Swan ☐
17. White-crowned Pigeon ☐
18. White Pelican ☐
19. White-tailed Ptarmigan ☐
20. Whooping Crane ☐

a. Arkansas National Wildlife Refuge, Texas
b. Chisos Mountains, Texas
c. Crest of the Rockies
d. Dry Tortugas, Florida
e. Edwards Plateau, Texas
f. Florida Bay
g. Florida Keys
h. Fortescue, New Jersey
i. Funk Island, Newfoundland
j. Lake Okeechobee, Florida
k. Martha's Vineyard, Massachusetts
l. Merritt Island, Florida
m. Michigan Jack Pine Country
n. Penikese Island, Massachusetts
o. Pyramid Lake, Nevada
p. Sable Island, Nova Scotia
q. Mt. Greylock, Massachusetts
r. Somewhere in Florida or Louisiana
s. Susquehanna River near Perryville, Maryland
t. Yellowstone Lake, Wyoming

MUTE SWAN

26

21. CHARACTERISTIC HABITATS—WATER BIRDS

Check the box or boxes with the right choice, or fill in the correct word. Each correct answer counts 5.

1. ☐ A boatman on the Missouri River or ☐ a locomotive engineer crossing the Rockies is more likely to see White Pelicans in migration.
2. A good place to see gulls is ☐ a railroad marshaling yard ☐ a sewer outlet.
3. Big Day route-makers plan to put the Least Bittern on the list when they hit ☐ a fresh-water marsh at dawn ☐ a salt marsh at high tide.
4. (E) From the sundeck of an Atlantic City boardwalk hotel would it be ☐ possible or ☐ impossible in spring or fall to see a Gannet?
5. (E) From the veranda of a southern mansion overlooking rice fields would you be more likely to see ☐ a Reddish or ☐ a Snowy Egret?
6. Gunners along the coast who hunt the Sora in fall usually head for ☐ fresh-water swamps ☐ salt or brackish marshes.
7. In looking for a Little Blue Heron would you go to a ☐ fresh-water marsh ☐ salt marsh or ☐ whichever is nearer?
8. In summer the Clapper Rail does its clapping primarily in a ☐ fresh-water marsh ☐ salt marsh.
9. (E) In summer the King Rail is king in a ☐ fresh-water marsh ☐ salt marsh.
10. Is the American Coot fussy about whether the water it swims in is fresh or salt? ☐ Yes ☐ No
11. (E) On a sandy beach one should look for a Great Cormorant ☐ at sea ☐ on piles or a rock jetty ☐ on the upper beach.
12. On a search for gallinules would one go to a ☐ salt marsh ☐ fresh-water marsh?
13. On January 1 you may start a new Year List. In order to put a grebe on this list would you visit unfrozen ☐ fresh water or ☐ salt water?
14. Suburbanites occasionally have a roost of ☐ Black-crowned ☐ Yellow-crowned Night Herons on their grounds.
15. The Black Rail likes ☐ the grassy edges of a fresh-water marsh ☐ a short-grass salt marsh ☐ a tall-grass salt marsh.
16. The Common Egret is common only in ☐ marshes (fresh-water or salt) ☐ mud flats.
17. (E) The motorist in Florida is most likely to see along a parkway shoulder a ☐ Cattle ☐ Common ☐ Snowy Egret.
18. What heron would you be most likely to flush if you were walking along a tiny ditch?_____
19. (W) Which cormorant, for nesting, prefers narrow ledges on steep cliffs? ☐ Brandt's ☐ Pelagic ☐ Red-faced
20. Would a beachcomber along the ocean front be ☐ likely ☐ unlikely to flush a Great Blue Heron?

22. CHARACTERISTIC HABITATS—GEESE AND DUCKS

Check the box or boxes below with the right choice. Each correct answer counts 5.

1. A bird watcher after a New Year's Eve party is more likely to see a ☐ Common Merganser ☐ Red-breasted Merganser as he drives home at dawn along the bay or beach.
2. A bird watcher in the Coast Guard could ☐ never ☐ often put a Cinnamon Teal on his list.
3. (E) Baymen along the Atlantic coast looking for Brant head for ☐ the ocean ☐ a bay.
4. Bird counters for the Audubon Christmas Census look for Blue-winged Teals on ☐ fresh-water ponds ☐ salt-water bays.
5. Canoeist escapees from a Junior Prom would be more likely to flush a pair of ☐ Ring-necked Ducks ☐ Canvasbacks from a wooded pond near the campus.
6. Coastal bird watchers in winter ☐ would ☐ would not be surprised to see a Green-winged Teal on salt water.
7. Hunters lie in wait for White-fronted Geese in blinds by ☐ deep ☐ shallow water.
8. Members of the Boston Tea Party would have been more likely, on their historic mission, to disturb a raft of sleeping ☐ Gadwall ☐ Greater Scaup.
9. One place you should never look for a Wood Duck is within sound of the sea. ☐ True ☐ False
10. On leaving home, Nantucket whalers probably encountered great rafts of Common Eiders ☐ near shore over the shoals ☐ as soon as their ship got into deep water.
11. Party-boat fishermen in winter ☐ never ☐ sometimes see Pintails on their way to their favorite fishing wrecks.
12. Ross' Goose indulges an appetite for grain in ☐ summer ☐ winter.
13. Surf fishermen in winter see (though they may not notice) many scaup. Are these more likely to be ☐ Greater ☐ Lesser?
14. (E) The Black Duck is a sportsman's favorite because ☐ it can be found in such a variety of places ☐ its habitat requirements are so restricted that it is a real challenge to find and kill one.
15. The Bufflehead in winter prefers ☐ the ocean ☐ southern mountain streams.
16. The Mallard ☐ will ☐ will not accept a variety of habitats.
17. When Henry Hudson sailed out of New York Harbor did he probably see any ☐ Shovelers or ☐ Oldsquaws in the Outer Bay?
18. When Jim Bridger made his summer trips through the Rocky Mountains could he have seen breeding Harlequin Ducks? ☐ Yes ☐ No
19. Woodland canoe-route campers are more likely to find a nesting pair of ☐ Hooded Mergansers ☐ Ruddy Ducks.
20. Would ☐ the Pilgrims or ☐ Captain John Smith have been more likely to see Harlequin Ducks?

23. CHARACTERISTIC HABITATS—SHOREBIRDS

Check the box or boxes with the right choice, or fill in the correct word. Each correct answer counts 5.

1. A ☐ Surfbird ☐ Western Sandpiper would be more likely to be on hand if a ship were driven ashore on a rocky western coast.
2. Bootleggers of the Prohibition era running liquor onto the Jersey coast would, in season, have disturbed migrating Whimbrel ☐ along the barrier beach ☐ in the salt marshes.
3. "By the shores of Gitche Gumee" could Hiawatha have seen a Spotted Sandpiper? ☐ Yes ☐ No
4. Fishermen on a rock jetty are most likely to see an ☐ American Golden Plover ☐ Black-bellied Plover ☐ Ruddy Turnstone.
5. Pioneers on the Oregon Trail must have seen many Long-billed Curlews on ☐ the mountains ☐ the prairies.
6. Sanitation engineers at sewage-disposal plants are more likely to see a ☐ Least ☐ Semipalmated Sandpiper.
7. The beachcomber of the outer beach sees the ☐ Least ☐ Semipalmated Sandpiper.
8. The Common Snipe prefers ☐ marshes ☐ swamps.
9. The Mountain Plover prefers ☐ deserts ☐ plains ☐ mountains.
10. The Pectoral Sandpiper prefers ☐ fields ☐ grassy marshes ☐ shallow pools.
11. The Semipalmated Plover prefers ☐ dry ☐ wet sand.
12. The Stilt Sandpiper prefers ☐ fields ☐ grassy marshes ☐ shallow pools.
13. Upland Plovers prefer ☐ airfields ☐ open cemeteries ☐ parking lots.
14. What shorebird is a golfer likely to see most often?_____

East only

15. In the old days when Coast Guards patrolled on foot, would they have been more likely on a sandy beach to flush ☐ an American Oystercatcher ☐ a Purple Sandpiper?
16. The American Woodcock prefers ☐ marshes ☐ swamps.
17. The Buff-breasted Sandpiper prefers ☐ fields ☐ grassy marshes ☐ shallow pools.
18. The Piping Plover prefers ☐ dry ☐ wet sand.

West only

19. Do clam diggers and Black Turnstones have the same habitat? ☐ Yes ☐ No
20. Do clam diggers and Black Oystercatchers have the same habitat? ☐ Yes ☐ No

24. HABITS—WATER BIRDS AND GAME BIRDS

Check the box or boxes with the right choice. Each correct answer counts 5.

1. Bobwhites roost ☐ on the ground in a circle facing out ☐ singly in bushes.
2. Gunners know that the White-winged Scoter usually travels ☐ alone ☐ in large flocks.
3. If the Ruddy Duck were an airplane, would it need ☐ a long ☐ a short runway?
4. If you were burying treasure, would you prefer the presence of ☐ a Buff-breasted Sandpiper ☐ a Greater Yellowlegs?
5. If you were burying more treasure, would you prefer the presence of ☐ a Black-necked Stilt ☐ a Hudsonian Godwit?
6. In an anserine walking race, would ☐ a goose ☐ a duck probably cross the finish line first?
7. In shallow water you would be more likely to see a ☐ Red ☐ Wilson's Phalarope tipping up for its food.
8. Most plovers try to lure intruders from their nests by feigning a broken wing. ☐ True ☐ False
9. (W) On rocky Pacific shores the great head-bobber is the ☐ Surfbird ☐ Wandering Tattler.
10. Persons lost in the North Woods can sometimes escape starvation by knocking over a ☐ Ruffed ☐ Spruce Grouse with a stick.
11. Surf fishermen on a rocky coast are more likely to observe ☐ Horned Grebes ☐ Pied-billed Grebes diving just beyond the surf.
12. The Black-bellied Plover acts more like ☐ a Chairman of the Board ☐ an indignant stockholder.
13. (E) The Greater Prairie Chicken is renowned for its ☐ unusually abbreviated ☐ elaborate courtship.
14. The ☐ Killdeer ☐ Mountain Plover is noted for a spectacular nuptial flight.
15. The Puritan Fathers soon learned that wild Turkeys roosted ☐ on the ground in a circle facing out ☐ in trees.
16. (E) The Purple Sandpiper is usually seen ☐ singly ☐ in pairs ☐ in groups of a dozen or more.
17. The Ruddy Turnstone ☐ does ☐ does not turn pebbles.
18. Visible borings in soft mud would suggest an ☐ American Golden Plover ☐ American Woodcock ☐ Eskimo Curlew.
19. (E) Which bird is the more wary? ☐ American Oystercatcher ☐ Wilson's Plover
20. Which bird is the most wary? ☐ Long-billed Curlew ☐ Baird's Sandpiper ☐ White-rumped Sandpiper

25. HABITS—BIRDS OF PREY AND OTHER LAND BIRDS

Check the box or boxes with the right choice. Each correct answer counts 5.

1. At night is the Turkey Vulture a solitary rooster? ☐ Yes ☐ No
2. Daniel Boone in the forests of Kentucky was more likely to have seen the ☐ Great Horned Owl ☐ Screech Owl hunting by day.
3. (E) Does the White-eyed Vireo forage ☐ higher ☐ lower than the Warbling?
4. In the *North Countree*, which owl is the more wary? ☐ Great Gray Owl ☐ Snowy Owl
5. (E) In the summer world of the leafy canopy, which vireo is the more sluggish? ☐ Red-eyed Vireo ☐ Yellow-throated Vireo
6. Is the ☐ Gray ☐ Hutton's Vireo the bigger flirter with its tail?
7. North Woods prowlers are more likely to see during the daytime the ☐ Boreal ☐ Saw-whet Owl.
8. On the lone prairie the Sage Thrasher is less wary than it is around ranches. ☐ True ☐ False
9. That "Bouncing (or Bobbing) Bet" on a rock is the ☐ Canyon ☐ Rock Wren.
10. The best owl-caller can never call up a Screech Owl closer than about 50 feet. ☐ True ☐ False
11. The Burrowing Owl is ☐ seldom ☐ usually seen by day.
12. The Osprey is most likely to lose the fish it has caught to a ☐ Bald ☐ Golden ☐ Gray Sea Eagle.
13. The Pigeon Hawk pumps its tail ☐ less ☐ more often than the Sparrow Hawk.
14. The shunpike motorist is likely to see a ☐ Gray-cheeked Thrush ☐ Eastern or Western Bluebird on a roadside wire.
15. Which bird would make the better emblem for a marriage-counseling service? ☐ Cedar Waxwing ☐ House Wren
16. Which pipit occurs in flocks? ☐ Sprague's Pipit ☐ Water Pipit
17. Which pipit wags its tail more? ☐ Sprague's Pipit ☐ Water Pipit
18. Which wren is the less secretive? ☐ Long-billed Marsh Wren ☐ Shore-billed Marsh Wren
19. Which wren is the more secretive ? ☐ House Wren ☐ Winter Wren
20. Would the ☐ Evening Grosbeak ☐ Cedar Waxwing make the better emblem for a temperance society?

26. HABITS—SPARROW FAMILY

Check the box or boxes with the right choice. Each correct answer counts 5.

1. Brewer's Sparrow is given to ☐ crepuscular ☐ meridional choruses.
2. ☐ Cassin's Finch ☐ Gray-crowned Rosy Finch feeds nearer to snow patches.
3. Pioneers on the Oregon Trail must many times have heard the song of the ☐ Lark Sparrow ☐ Rufous-winged Sparrow given from an elevated perch or while hovering in the air.
4. A Hudson Bay trapper following his trapline might see the ☐ Fox Sparrow ☐ Pine Grosbeak bathing in soft snow.
5. The Black-throated Sparrow forages ☐ high ☐ low.
6. The ☐ Cassin's Sparrow ☐ Botteri's Sparrow utters a flight song while fluttering up several feet with its head up and wings outspread.
7. The home-loving male ☐ Blue Grosbeak ☐ Rose-breasted Grosbeak sometimes sings on his nest.
8. The Vesper Sparrow sings most at ☐ dawn ☐ dusk ☐ midday.
9. The White-crowned Sparrow acts more like the ☐ lord ☐ serf of the manor.
10. Which bird behaves more like a parrot? ☐ Red Crossbill ☐ Rufous-sided Towhee
11. Which bird fans its tail more often? ☐ Green-tailed Towhee ☐ Rufous-sided Towhee
12. Which three of the following often flock together in winter? ☐ Crossbills ☐ Redpolls ☐ Siskins ☐ Longspurs ☐ Three-toed Woodpeckers
13. Which bird would make the better trade-mark for a child's snowsuit? ☐ Slate-colored Junco ☐ Savannah Sparrow
14. Which sparrow would make the better emblem for an orchestra? ☐ Tree Sparrow ☐ Chipping Sparrow

East only

15. Drivers in convertibles along the Blue Ridge Parkway in summer would expect to see many ☐ Indigo Buntings ☐ Painted Buntings singing from dead roadside branches.
16. The Ipswich Sparrow often associates with which three of the following? ☐ Horned Larks ☐ Longspurs ☐ Robins ☐ Snow Buntings ☐ Towhees ☐ Woodpeckers
17. The ☐ Sharp-tailed Sparrow ☐ Seaside Sparrow sometimes wades to its belly.
18. Transcontinental motorists in summer on the plains should commonly encounter the ☐ Dickcissel ☐ Le Conte's Sparrow.

West only

19. Like royal courtiers, the members of a mated pair of ☐ Abert's Towhees ☐ Brown Towhees engage in a brief bowing ceremony on rejoining each other.
20. Motorists in western National Parks should not be surprised to see a ☐ Black-headed Grosbeak ☐ Rose-breasted Grosbeak at their picnic table.

27. IDENTIFICATION ON GROUND OR PERCH—
WATER BIRDS

Check the box or boxes with the right choice, or fill in the correct word. Each correct answer counts 5.

1. Does the Common Egret, when feeding, rush about erratically like the Snowy Egret?_____
2. Does the Common Snipe make any use of its protective coloration? _____
3. Is the Greater Yellowlegs ☐ more or ☐ less of a Rotarian than the Lesser Yellowlegs?
4. Is the ☐ Pied-billed Grebe or the ☐ Gannet more helpless on land?
5. Name two species of birds that walk on lily pads. 1._____
   2._____
6. The Green Heron never alights on trees in the breeding season. ☐ True ☐ False
7. The Least Bittern ☐ often ☐ seldom alights in trees in the breeding season.
8. The Ruddy Turnstone ☐ always ☐ never ☐ sometimes perches off the ground.
9. What shorebird probes the mud like a sewing machine with its bill at an angle?_____
10. What shorebird probes the mud like a sewing machine with its bill perpendicular?_____
11. Which bob the head? ☐ Lesser Yellowlegs ☐ Solitary Sandpiper ☐ Stilt Sandpiper
12. Which bird can walk with less difficulty? ☐ Common Loon ☐ Red-throated Loon
13. Which bird feeds in deeper water? ☐ Semipalmated Sandpiper ☐ Western Sandpiper
14. Which of these terms applies best to the Upland Plover? ☐ Democrat ☐ Republican ☐ Mugwump

East only

15. In deportment does Wilson's Plover suggest a ☐ senator or a ☐ page boy?
16. Spreadeagled wings when perched are characteristic of the ☐ Anhinga ☐ Limpkin.
17. What member of the heron family occasionally perches on the backs of cattle?_____
18. Which bird moves around faster when feeding? ☐ Little Blue Heron ☐ Snowy Egret
19. Which bird, when alarmed, is easier to see? ☐ American Bittern ☐ Louisiana Heron
20. Which bird, when fishing, acts more like a drunken sailor? ☐ Great Blue Heron ☐ Reddish Egret

28. IDENTIFICATION ON GROUND OR PERCH—
GAME BIRDS AND OTHER LAND BIRDS

Check the box or boxes with the right choice. Each correct answer
counts 5.

1. Can Mr. Headdown, the White-breasted Nuthatch, also climb up
a tree head first? ☐ Yes ☐ No
2. (W) Do pairs of California Quail roost privately when courting?
☐ Yes ☐ No
3. (E) Does the Carolina Wren ☐ bob up and down or ☐ teeter?
4. (W) Is the Blue Grouse in winter a ☐ snow-rooster or a ☐tree-
rooster?
5. Is the Ring-necked Pheasant, a ☐ ground-rooster or a ☐ tree-
rooster?
6. (E) Le Conte's Sparrow seeks safety ☐ in flight ☐ in running
away.
7. (W) Male ☐ Chukar Partridges ☐ Sharp-tailed Grouse often crow
from a rocky outpoint at dawn.
8. Most members of which of these groups are able to perch upside
down while feeding? ☐ Bushtits ☐ Chickadees ☐ Titmice
9. Ptarmigan somehow always manage to find a snowless area in
which to roost. ☐ True ☐ False
10. The California and Sage Thrashers prefer to seek safety ☐ in
flight ☐ in running.
11. The Chipping Sparrow and Indigo Bunting sing from a ☐ high
☐ low perch.
12. The Dipper appears to walk ☐ on ☐ through ☐ under the water.
13. The Fox Sparrow scratches noisily with ☐ one foot at a time
☐ both feet at once.
14. The lizard-eating Roadrunner can run up to ☐ 8 ☐ 18 ☐ 28 m.p.h.
15. The Mockingbird ☐ never ☐ seldom ☐ often feeds on the ground.
16. The Rufous-crowned Sparrow and Rufous-sided Towhee sing from
a ☐ high ☐ low perch.
17. The Starling ☐ never ☐ occasionally ☐ often perches on a tele-
vision aerial.
18. Which jay on alighting often bows in different directions? ☐ Gray
Jay ☐ Scrub Jay
19. Which quail seeks safety by running with neck outstretched and
topknot erect? ☐ Bobwhite ☐ Scaled Quail
20. Which bird nods its head as it walks? ☐ Brewer's Blackbird
☐ Redwinged Blackbird

29. HOPPERS AND WALKERS

Which of these hop? Which walk? Put an X in the correct column. If a bird both hops *and* walks put an X in each column. Each correct answer counts 5.

Species	Hops	Walks
1. Boat-tailed Grackle	_____	_____
2. Brown-headed Cowbird	_____	_____
3. Clark's Nutcracker	_____	_____
4. Common Crow	_____	_____
5. Horned Lark	_____	_____
6. House Sparrow	_____	_____
7. Magpie (in a hurry)	_____	_____
8. Piñon Jay	_____	_____
9. Redwinged Blackbird	_____	_____
10. Robin	_____	_____
11. Rusty Blackbird	_____	_____
12. Savannah Sparrow	_____	_____
13. Snow Bunting	_____	_____
14. Starling	_____	_____
15. Steller's Jay	_____	_____
16. Vesper Sparrow	_____	_____

East only

Species	Hops	Walks
17. Blue Jay	_____	_____
18. Brown Thrasher	_____	_____
19. Common Grackle	_____	_____
20. Ipswich Sparrow	_____	_____

DIPPER

30. IDENTIFICATION OF DUCKS, GEESE, AND SWANS

Check the box or boxes with the right choice, or fill in the correct word. Each correct answer counts 5.

1. A boat that sits low in the water would be more appropriately named the ☐ Widgeon ☐ Gadwall.
2. A duck that pivots as it feeds is more likely to be ☐ an American Widgeon ☐ a Shoveler.
3. An advertising agency artist wishes to use a duck to suggest great speed in flight. Should he use a ☐ Green-winged Teal ☐ Canvasback?
4. (E) A V-shaped flying wedge is more likely to be ☐ Brant ☐ White-fronted Geese.
5. Ducks with a heavy-looking flight low over salt water are ☐ Black Ducks ☐ Common Eiders.
6. (W) Emperor Geese in migration fly high and ☐ abreast ☐ in long lines.
7. Flocks of what sea duck veer like shorebirds in flight, and thus make an alternate dark and light pattern?_____
8. If a high seat on the water were a sign of dominance, would the ☐ male or the ☐ female Common Goldeneye "rule the roost"?
9. (E) If a high seat on the water were a sign of good breeding would the ☐ Mute Swan or the ☐ Whistling Swan be the better bred?
10. If flight were typical of temperament would the ☐ Canvasback or the ☐ Redhead have the more even disposition?
11. On the water, Brant, Pintail, Wood Duck, and Harlequin Duck sit ☐ high ☐ low.
12. On the water, the only scoter to hold its bill horizontal or uplifted is the_____.
13. Swans fly in ☐ V-shaped wedges ☐ irregular lines with their necks ☐ extended ☐ drawn in.
14. The flight of what small duck suggests remotely that of a bumblebee?_____
15. (E) The neck is arched in the Mute Swan, erect in the Whistling Swan. ☐ True ☐ False
16. The Ruddy Duck and Common Merganser can ☐ sink slowly ☐ dive abruptly ☐ do both.
17. The Shoveler sits ☐ high ☐ low in the water.
18. The Snow Goose flies in ☐ regular V's ☐ loose V's ☐ irregular bunches.
19. The wings of what species of duck whistle noisily in flight?_____
20. Which duck has the faster wingbeat? ☐ Gadwall ☐ Mallard

31. IDENTIFICATION IN FLIGHT—WATER BIRDS

Mark the right answer by checking the appropriate box or filling in the blank. Each correct answer counts 5.

1. Loons have a ☐ faster ☐ slower wingbeat than ducks.
2. Must a grebe patter along the surface of the water before taking flight? ☐ Yes ☐ No
3. The Common Loon on the water usually escapes by ☐ diving ☐ flight.
4. The feet and *part of the legs* of the ☐ Black-crowned Night Heron ☐ Yellow-crowned Night Heron project behind its tail in flight. With the other species, only the feet project behind.
5. Very high overhead the ☐ Brown Pelican ☐ White Pelican engages in beautiful aerial soaring.
6. What heron in flight looks, at a distance, like a crow?_____
7. What member of the heron family in flight is noted for its buff wing-patches?_____
8. What member of the heron family in flight is noted for the black primaries on its brown wings?_____
9. Which birds fly with their heads and necks drooping? ☐ Common Loon ☐ Red-necked Grebe ☐ Red-breasted Merganser
10. Which bird has slower wingbeats? ☐ Common Egret ☐ Snowy Egret
11. Which heron in flight looks somewhat like a short-necked gull? _____
12. Which loon can spring into the air without pattering? ☐ Arctic Loon ☐ Red-throated Loon
13. Which loon in migration is most apt to be seen circling on set wings high overhead? ☐ Arctic Loon ☐ Common Loon ☐ Red-throated Loon

East only

14. The petrel with the nighthawklike flight is ☐ Leach's ☐ Wilson's.
15. The petrel with the swallowlike flight is ☐ Leach's ☐ Wilson's.
16. Which cormorant has slower wingbeats? ☐ Double-crested Cormorant ☐ Great Cormorant
17. Which flaps its wings more? ☐ Fulmar ☐ Greater Shearwater
18. Which petrel is a ship-follower? ☐ Leach's Petrel ☐ Wilson's Petrel
19. Which shearwater flaps more and glides less? ☐ Audubon's Shearwater ☐ Manx Shearwater

West only

20. The Pale-footed Shearwater has a slower wingbeat than the Sooty Shearwater. ☐ True ☐ False

32. IDENTIFICATION IN FLIGHT—BIRDS OF PREY

Match the species with the flight characteristic and answer the other questions by placing the appropriate letter in the box. Each correct answer counts 5.

Characteristic	Species
1. A buteo noted for its hovering, sometimes hangs motionless in air on an updraft	a. Black Hawk
2. A falcon noted for its hovering	b. Broad-winged Hawk, Swainson's Hawk
3. Courses low over the plains with its wings in an open V	c. Everglade Kite (E)
4. Dives into water	d. Marsh Hawk
5. Eats snake in midair	e. Mississippi Kite (E)
6. Flaps 4 or 5 times then glides	f. Osprey
7. Flaps slowly just over top of marsh grass looking for snails	g. Peregrine Falcon
8. Flight suggests that of Black Vulture but bird sometimes engages in spectacular dives to earth (Southwest)	h. Rough-legged Hawk
9. Has a buoyant, gull-like flight and often tilts its long, black tail to show two-toned upper surface of its wings	i. Sharp-shinned Hawk, Cooper's Hawk
10. Has a buoyant, gull-like flight and often tilts its long, angled wings as it quarters low over the marsh	j. Sparrow Hawk
11. Has long, pointed wings held upward in flight but with the tips pointing down; often hovers and dangles its legs in flight	k. Swainson's Hawk
12. Hundreds circle high in air in migration	l. Swallow-tailed Kite (E)
13. Like Turkey Vulture in angle of wings and in habit of balancing when soaring (Southwest)	m. White-tailed Kite
14. Renowned for its swooping	n. Zone-tailed Hawk

15. Harlan's Hawk has a swifter flight than the Red-tailed Hawk.
☐ True ☐ False
16. Swainson's Hawk has a more rapid wingbeat than the Red-tailed Hawk. ☐ True ☐ False
17. The Bald Eagle has a more rapid wingbeat than the Golden Eagle. ☐ True ☐ False
18. The Gyrfalcon has a swifter flight than the Peregrine Falcon. ☐ True ☐ False
19. The Red-shouldered Hawk has a more buoyant flight than the Red-tailed Hawk. ☐ True ☐ False
20. Which is the hoverer? ☐ Bald Eagle ☐ Osprey

33. IDENTIFICATION IN FLIGHT—LAND BIRDS

Check the appropriate box or boxes, or fill in the correct word. Each correct answer counts 5.

1. The ☐ Catbird ☐ Northern Shrike drops from its perch, flies close to the ground, then swoops upward to its next perch.
2. The Yellow-headed Blackbird flies in ☐ long ☐ wide flocks.
3. Which bluebird is given to hovering? ☐ Eastern Bluebird ☐ Western Bluebird ☐ Mountain Bluebird
4. What mountain-stream bird has a buzzy, quail-like flight?_____
5. Which nuthatch sometimes catches insects in air? ☐ Red-breasted Nuthatch ☐ White-breasted Nuthatch
6. Which thrush flies with widespread, slow-beating wings reminiscent of Say's Phoebe? ☐ Townsend's Solitaire ☐ Wheatear
7. Which thrush flits from rock to rock, snatches insects in the air, and sometimes hovers? ☐ Townsend's Solitaire ☐ Wheatear
8. Which bird is more noted for the aerial evolutions of its flocks? ☐ Redwinged Blackbird ☐ Starling
9. Which of these birds sometimes catches insects in air? ☐ Blue-gray Gnatcatcher ☐ Brown Creeper
10. Which three of these adjectives best describe the flight of the Water Pipit? ☐ Buoyant ☐ Clumsy ☐ Direct ☐ Erratic ☐ Undulating
11. Which two thrushes, when flushed, fly to a low branch, remain motionless, then flit on farther if disturbed again? ☐ Gray-cheeked Thrush ☐ Swainson's Thrush ☐ Wood Thrush
12. Which warbler sings in air with feet dangling?_____

East only

13. The ☐ Common Grackle ☐ Redwinged Blackbird has a direct, horizontal flight toward its roost.
14. The ☐ Long-billed Marsh Wren ☐ Short-billed Marsh Wren often rises 6 to 10 feet in the air from a stalk and flutters down, singing.
15. The ☐ Philadelphia Vireo ☐ Red-eyed Vireo sometimes catches insects in air.
16. Which of these, if flushed, will flit to a low bush and sit motionless? ☐ Connecticut Warbler ☐ American Redstart
17. Which two warblers have a somewhat similar flight? ☐ Cerulean Warbler ☐ Prothonotary Warbler ☐ Hooded Warbler ☐ Northern Waterthrush

West only

18. Which species almost always occurs in loose flocks of up to 50 or more that progress irregularly as members straggle from tree to tree singly or in small groups? ☐ Black-tailed Gnatcatcher ☐ Common Bushtit
19. Which vireo engages in more short flights and hops through the shrub and tree canopy than other vireos? ☐ Gray Vireo ☐ Hutton's Vireo
20. Which looks remotely like a big butterfly with its slow wingbeat and fluttering flight? ☐ Phainopepla ☐ Pyrrhuloxia

34. BIRD VOICES—ENGLISH WORDS AND PHRASES

These words or phrases suggest the voices of certain species of birds which are listed in the column on the right. Match the species and the description by putting the appropriate letter in the box. Each correct answer counts 5.

Description

1. A clear, whistled *dear dear dear*, normally three or four times, de-descending the scale ☐
2. A complaining *shriek, shriek* (Cruickshank) ☐
3. A high, nasal *ink, ink, ink* like a little tin horn ☐
4. A loud whistle, *quick THREE BEERS!* ☐
5. A nasal, rasping *escape, escape* ☐
6. A repetition of little phrases, remotely robinlike, *now you see me, now you don't, here I am, there I go* ☐
7. A soft mellow warble, *purity purity* ☐
8. A squeaky *do oil me*, like a rusty hinge ☐
9. A sweet, sometimes nostalgic, *spring-o'-the YEar* ☐
10. A sweet, whistled *SPRING'S come*, the first note higher ☐
11. A tremulous wail, descending, or all on one key, *oh-o-o-o that I had never been bor-or-or-or-orn* (Thoreau) ☐

Species

a. Black-capped Chickadee, Carolina Chickadee
b. Common Snipe
c. Eastern Bluebird
d. Eastern Meadowlark
e. Greater Yellowlegs
f. Olive-sided Flycatcher
g. Osprey
h. Red-breasted Nuthatch
i. Red-eyed Vireo
j. Rusty Blackbird
k. Screech Owl

East only

12. A clear, whistled *tea-kettle tea-kettle tea-kettle* ☐
13. A creaky *side light, side light* ☐
14. A distinctive, nasal *three-eight* ☐
15. A dreamy *trees, trees, murm'ring trees (murm'ring* lower) ☐
16. A loud, ringing *turtle, turtle, turtle* ☐
17. A thin, wiry, *we see, we see, we see* spiraling upward ☐
18. *Pleased, pleased, pleased t'MEET-cha* ☐
19. Thoreau wrote it as *drop it, drop it, cover it, cover it, I'll pull it up, I'll pull it up* ☐
20. *Who cooks for you? Who cooks for you-all?* ☐

East only

l. Yellow-throated Vireo
m. Barred Owl
n. Black-and-white Warbler
o. Black-throated Green Warbler
p. Blue Jay
q. Brown Thrasher
r. Carolina Wren
s. Chestnut-sided Warbler
t. Kentucky Warbler

35. BIRD VOICES—SOUNDS

Match the species with the description by placing the appropriate letter in the box. Each correct answer counts 5.

Description

1. A croaking *c-r-r-r-u-u-k* ☐
2. (E) A distinctive, easy-to-learn *zee-zee-zee-zee-zee-zee*, rising in pitch throughout ☐
3. A harsh *TOOOOT-toot*, like an antique automobile horn ☐
4. A harsh *ca ca ca*, higher than Common Crow ☐
5. A high, penetrating *zee zee zee ZEE ZEE zee zee zee*, of even pitch, becoming louder in middle, fading away at end ☐
6. A high-pitched, loud *killy, killy, killy* ☐
7. A long, thin, high *tseee*, longer than Golden-crowned Kinglet's and not quickly repeated in series ☐
8. A loud, rhythmic *yuk-yuk-yuk* ☐
9. A loud, wild rattle usually heard in flight ☐
10. A musical, gabbling *south, south, southerly* or *how doodle do* ☐
11. An emphatic *che-BEC*, much repeated ☐
12. (E) An unhurried, liquid, bell-like melody *"eeohlay-ayolee-ahleelee-ayleahlolah-ilolilee"* (Saunders) ☐
13. A series of hollow *whree-u*'s descending the scale ☐
14. A shrill, high-pitched, scolding *spee, spee, spee* ☐
15. A thin, high hiss ☐
16. (E) A wild, raucous *wheap* from the woods ☐
17. A wooden *kuk kuk kuk kow kow kow*, the last three notes retarded ☐
18. (E) Like the song of a hoarse robin ☐
19. (E) Like the yelping of a pack of hounds ☐
20. Sounds like the French word *tiens!*

Species

a. Belted Kingfisher
b. Black-billed Magpie
c. Blackpoll Warbler
d. Black Skimmer
e. Blue-gray Gnatcatcher
f. Brown Creeper
g. Cedar Waxwing
h. Common Raven
i. Flicker (Yellow-shafted or Red-shafted)
j. Flicker (Yellow-shafted or Red-shafted)
k. Great Crested Flycatcher
l. Least Flycatcher
m. Oldsquaw
n. Prairie Warbler
o. Ring-necked Pheasant
p. Scarlet Tanager
q. Sparrow Hawk
r. Veery
s. Wood Thrush
t. Yellow-billed Cuckoo

36. NESTS AND EGGS BY FAMILIES

Certain families of birds have highly characteristic nests and eggs. Match the descriptions on the right with the families on the left by placing the appropriate letter in the box. *A.O.U. Check-list* species only. Each correct answer counts 5.

Families

1. Auks ☐
2. Chickadees ☐
3. Chickenlike Birds ☐
4. Cormorants ☐
5. Cranes ☐
6. Grebes ☐
7. Herons and Egrets ☐
8. Hummingbirds ☐
9. Jaegers ☐
10. Loons ☐
11. Nuthatches ☐
12. Owls ☐
13. Plovers and Sandpipers ☐
14. Rails ☐
15. Shearwaters and Petrels ☐
16. Sparrows ☐
17. Terns ☐
18. Vireos ☐
19. Vultures ☐
20. Woodpeckers ☐

Description

a. A depression in the sand or ground, usually scantily lined, 3 to 4 pear-shaped eggs (with rare exceptions)
b. A depression in the sand, or of vegetation in a marsh; in colonies; 2 to 3 eggs
c. A hole in a decayed stump, branch, or birdbox
d. A platform in the marsh, sometimes more elaborate, 6 to 12 eggs
e. Dainty, cuplike, hung from one fork of a twig
f. Eggs white, almost round
g. Exquisite, tiny, cup-shaped, covered with lichens, made of plant down
h. Floating masses of vegetation
i. In a burrow or rock crevice on an island, except for one species which nests in the open
j. In a cavity which the bird often excavates itself in a dead stump or branch
k. In a hole which the bird excavates itself in a tree; eggs white; (sometimes nests in birdbox)
l. In a hollow log or crevice in rocks, or under a thick bush
m. Of grass rootlets and stems on, or near, the ground, 3 to 6 eggs
n. Of sticks, usually high in trees, in colonies
o. Of mud and vegetation by fresh water
p. On a ledge, or in a rock crevice or burrow, in colonies; eggs often pear-shaped
q. On the ground or in trees on a rocky island or ledge
r. On the ground, 6 to 15 eggs
s. On the ground, usually 2 eggs
t. On the tundra or a rocky ledge, 2 to 3 eggs

37. IDENTIFICATION BY RANGE AND SEASON— WATER BIRDS

Check the appropriate box or fill in the blank. Each correct answer counts 5.

1. A night heron in upstate New York would almost certainly be a ☐ Black-crowned ☐ Yellow-crowned.
2. Eastern visitors on their way to the Yellowstone sometimes see breeding pairs of ☐ Greater Scaup ☐ Lesser Scaup in eastern Wyoming.
3. Late fall beachcombers on the Virginia coast might well see an ☐ American Golden Plover ☐ Black-bellied Plover.
4. Polar Bear Club bathers on Cape Cod might see a ☐ Sanderling ☐ Semipalmated Sandpiper.
5. The only big tern regularly seen in Nova Scotia is the ☐ Caspian ☐ Royal.
6. The only eagle in Florida is the_____Eagle.
7. The only summer grebe in Indiana is the ☐ Eared ☐ Pied-billed.
8. The only vulture regularly seen in Minnesota is the_____.
9. The summer gull with a black head in Montana is the ☐ Black-headed ☐ Franklin's ☐ Laughing.
10. The wintering Yellowlegs on the Oregon coast is a ☐ Greater ☐ Lesser.
11. Summer travelers on their way through Alberta sometimes see breeding pairs of ☐ Common Scoters ☐ White-winged Scoters.
12. Trappers in northern Ontario might well see a ☐ Rock Ptarmigan ☐ Willow Ptarmigan.
13. When the Swedes landed on Delaware Bay in the 1600's they probably ☐ did ☐ did not see Arctic Terns.

East only

14. A bird-watcher lifeguard on the New Jersey coast on Memorial Day saw a flock of ☐ Double-crested Cormorants ☐ Great Cormorants fly by.
15. An ibis seen in Western Florida would almost certainly be the ☐ Glossy ☐ White-faced.
16. A winter buteo in the United States (except Florida) will not be a ☐ Broad-winged Hawk ☐ Swainson's Hawk ☐ Harlan's Hawk.
17. Farmers in Manitoba in late summer often see "white herons." Are they ☐ Common Egrets ☐ immature Little Blue Herons or ☐ Snowy Egrets?
18. The only true ibis in New Mexico is the_____.
19. Upland gunners in Missouri might flush a ☐ Greater Prairie Chicken ☐ Lesser Prairie Chicken.

West only

20. In 1846 a flock of ☐ California Gulls ☐ Franklin's Gulls suddenly descended and ate vast numbers of grasshoppers that were devouring the crops of the infant Mormon Colony at the Great Salt Lake in Utah.

38. ORNITHOLOGICAL TERMS

These are words frequently used in ornithology relating to plumage, structure or habits. Match the word and the meaning by placing the appropriate letter in the box. Each correct answer counts 5.

<u>Ornithological Terms</u>

1. Albinism ☐
2. Altricial ☐
3. Auriculars ☐
4. Axillars ☐
5. Carinate ☐
6. Cere ☐
7. Crepuscular ☐
8. Erythrism ☐
9. Lores ☐
10. Maxilla
11. Melanism ☐
12. Nape ☐
13. Precocial ☐
14. Ratite ☐
15. Rectrices ☐
16. Primaries ☐
17. Remiges ☐
18. Superciliary ☐
19. Tarsus ☐
20. Zygodactyl ☐

<u>Meaning</u>

a. Abnormal absence of color
b. Back of the neck
c. Feathers around the ear
d. Flight feathers
e. Over the eye
f. Part of foot between ankle-joint and toes, looks like shank or leg
g. Pertaining to twilight
h. Primaries plus secondaries
i. Soft basal cover of maxilla
j. Spaces between eyes and bill
k. Tail feathers
l. Two toes forward, two toes back
m. Upper mandible
n. Wingpit feathers
o. With a flat sternum
p. With a keeled sternum
q. With an excess of black coloration
r. With an excess of red coloration
s. Young able to run around on hatching
t. Young helpless on hatching

FOR THE EXPERT

Adult

Immature

SNOWY OWL

39. CHARACTERISTIC HABITATS—BIRDS OF PREY

Check the appropriate box. Each correct answer counts 5.

1. A summer forest ranger in the White Mountains, if a bird watcher, should be able to put ☐ a Saw-whet Owl ☐ a Snowy Owl on his list.
2. Canoeists in the north woods sometimes flush a ☐ Harris' Hawk ☐ Goshawk from a big evergreen.
3. Driving through the Badlands National Monument, bird watchers keep on the lookout for a ☐ Bald Eagle ☐ Ferruginous Hawk.
4. Feuding Appalachian mountaineers are more likely to see ☐ Great Horned Owls ☐ Short-eared Owls.
5. Johnny Tremaine would have been more likely to disturb a ☐ Barn Owl ☐ Great Horned Owl in the belfry of Boston's Old North Church
6. New York Linnaean Society members often find ☐ Long-eared Owls ☐ Short-eared Owls in pine groves at Jones Beach, Long Island.
7. On a bird trip you enter some moist woods. Is such a tract better for a ☐ Red-shouldered Hawk or a ☐ Red-tailed Hawk?
8. On a Christmas count would you look for an accipiter in ☐ deep woods ☐ the open ☐ wood edges?
9. Protectors of the Bald Eagle search for nest sites to guard ☐ in rugged upland country ☐ near water.
10. The Golden Eagle in North America prefers the Wild Blue Yonder over ☐ the mountains ☐ the coast.
11. The Red-shouldered Hawk is more often found in larger wood lots than the Red-tailed Hawk. ☐ True ☐ False
12. The Swamp Fox, Francis Marion, and his men must have been very familiar with the call of the ☐ Barred Owl ☐ Spotted Owl.
13. The wide, open spaces of the plains and prairies are poor places to see Harlan's Hawk. ☐ True ☐ False
14. Timber cruisers in dense woods are more likely to see a ☐ Great Gray Owl ☐ Hawk Owl.

East only

15. The Big Cypress country of southern Florida attracts the bird watcher who needs for his life list the ☐ Everglade Kite ☐ Short-tailed Hawk.
16. Walking through the greenwood of a May morning in the Northeast, a bird watcher noticed a small buteo hawk on a branch. It was a ☐ Broad-winged Hawk ☐ Short-tailed Hawk.

West only

17. Clementine's father might well have heard ☐ an Elf Owl ☐ a Spotted Owl near his cavern.
18. In her girlhood, Evangeline, in a hard winter, might have seen around her father's farm a ☐ Boreal Owl ☐ Elf Owl.
19. In the Saguaro National Monument you can pretty well count on ☐ an Elf Owl ☐ a Pigmy Owl.
20. The Whiskered Owl prefers ☐ deep woods ☐ canyons.

40. CHARACTERISTIC HABITATS—GULLS AND TERNS

Check the appropriate box or boxes. Each correct answer counts 5.

GULLS

1. Arctic explorers along the edge of the pack ice in winter expect to see the ☐ Ivory Gull ☐ Sabine's Gull.
2. At a Great Lakes harbor in winter you might possibly see a ☐ Glaucous-winged Gull ☐ Little Gull ☐ Ross' Gull.
3. High over a large city you would be more likely to see flying a ☐ Glaucous Gull ☐ Herring Gull ☐ Iceland Gull.
4. If your transpolar plane crash-landed in the High Arctic in winter the sight of which of these gulls would be less unlikely? ☐ Ross' Gull ☐ Sabine's Gull.
5. In the northern coniferous forest in summer you would be more likely to find a ☐ Black-legged Kittiwake ☐ Bonaparte's Gull ☐ Little Gull.
6. Near a pig trough in the interior you would be more likely to see a ☐ California Gull ☐ Mew Gull ☐ Ring-billed Gull.
7. On the inland prairies in summer you might well see a ☐ Bonaparte's Gull ☐ Franklin's Gull ☐ Heermann's Gull.
8. Which of these gulls is a marsh breeder? ☐ Ring-billed Gull ☐ Laughing Gull.

East only

9. At a sewer outlet along the Atlantic Coast in winter you would be more likely to see a ☐ Black-headed Gull ☐ Ivory Gull ☐ Laughing Gull.
10. Crossing the North Atlantic in midwinter you might well see far from shore a ☐ Bonaparte's Gull ☐ Glaucous Gull ☐ Mew Gull.

West only

11. When nesting on the same cliffs with the Black-legged Kittiwake, the Red-legged Kittiwake occupies the ☐ lower ☐ upper ledges.

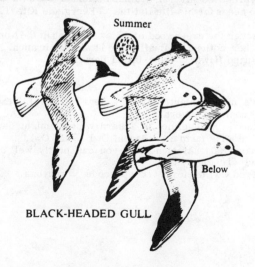

Summer

Below

BLACK-HEADED GULL

TERNS

12. A common tern of the prairie slough is the ☐ Black Tern ☐ Caspian Tern ☐ Gull-billed Tern.
13. Forster's Tern prefers ☐ coastal islands ☐ marshes ☐ rocky coasts.
14. Picnickers on the shores of certain large interior lakes might see a ☐ Caspian Tern ☐ Royal Tern.
15. The Gull-billed Tern prefers ☐ coastal islands ☐ marshes ☐ rocky coasts.

East only

16. Hikers along shorelines in the interior often see ☐ Least Terns ☐ Roseate Terns.
17. In Newfoundland, where both Arctic and Common Terns occur, the Arctic Tern prefers the ☐ coast and inner islands ☐ outer islands; the Common prefers the other.
18. On coastal islands when you find Royal Terns you also look for ☐ Arctic Terns ☐ Black Terns ☐ Sandwich Terns.
19. Which of these will a camper on an interior lake in northern Canada be more likely to see? ☐ Arctic Tern ☐ Roseate Tern
20. Yachtsmen cruising at sea in the subtropics expect to see the ☐ Least Tern ☐ Roseate Tern ☐ Sooty Tern.

COMMON TERN   ARCTIC TERN   ROSEATE TERN

41. CHARACTERISTIC HABITATS—LAND BIRDS

Check the appropriate box or fill in the right key letter. Each correct answer counts 5.

Woodpeckers

1. A shut-in is more likely to see a ☐ Downy Woodpecker ☐ Ladder-backed Woodpecker ☐ Hairy Woodpecker.
2. On a big, bare tree by an open field would you usually be more likely to see a ☐ Lewis' Woodpecker or a ☐ Pileated Woodpecker?

East only

3. The favorite habitat of the Red-cockaded Woodpecker is a group of loblolly pines between 40 and 50 years old. ☐ True ☐ False
4. "This is the forest primeval, the murmuring pines and the hemlocks." Would such country be better for a ☐ Black-backed Three-toed Woodpecker or for a ☐ Golden-fronted Woodpecker?
5. Will a ☐ logger or an ☐ apple grower see more Red-headed Woodpeckers?

Empidonaxes

Empidonax flycatchers look very much alike, but each of the 9 species has its own favorite breeding habitat. Match the habitat with the species.

Species	Breeding Habitat
6. Dusky ☐	a. Arid brushlands
7. Traill's ☐	b. Chaparral, forest openings
8. Western ☐	c. Deciduous and mixed woods

East only

9. Acadian ☐	d. In Northeast, alder swamps; in Midwest, dry uplands
10. Least ☐	e. Middle altitudes in southwestern mountains
11. Yellow-bellied ☐	f. Mountain forests in West

West only

12. Buff-breasted ☐	g. Northern coniferous forest
13. Gray ☐	h. Rural countryside
14. Hammond's ☐	i. Woods near water, beeches; Southeast

LADDER-BACKED WOODPECKER

41. CHARACTERISTIC HABITATS—LAND BIRDS *(Continued)*

Sparrows

Sparrows are often troublesome to identify; many of them look much alike. But their habitat preferences are quite distinctive. Match the habitat with the species.

15. Baird's ☐   j. Arid country with sparse grasses and cacti

16. Botteri's ☐   k. Brushy coastal prairie

17. Brewer's ☐   l. Dry long-grass prairie

18. Cassin's ☐   m. Northern bogs

19. Lincoln's ☐   n. Prairie marshes

East only

20. Le Conte's ☐   o. Sagebrush

42. HABITS—WATER BIRDS, GAME BIRDS, BIRDS OF PREY

Check the appropriate box or boxes. Each correct answer counts 5.

Water Birds

1. A merganser is seen with its tail cocked. Is it a ☐ Hooded or a ☐ Red-breasted?
2. (E) If a Whistling Swan in migration came down into the same pond with a Mute Swan, which would spend more time tipping and feeding from the bottom? ☐ Mute Swan ☐ Whistling Swan
3. If silence, in the goose world, were a virtue, would ☐ the Ross' Goose or ☐ the Snow Goose be the more virtuous?
4. Is the American Golden Plover more aggressive than the Black-bellied? ☐ Yes ☐ No
5. The Pectoral Sandpiper seeks safety by ☐ early flight ☐ lying close.
6. The Red Phalarope, while feeding, makes more dabs per second with its bill than does the Northern. ☐ True ☐ False
7. (W) The ☐ Ruddy Turnstone ☐ Surfbird digs broad shallow holes in the sand.
8. You would be more likely to see a ☐ Northern Phalarope ☐ Wilson's Phalarope running about on floating seaweed.

Game Birds

9. Eskimos look for roosting Rock Ptarmigan ☐ on a rock ☐ on a willow ☐ in the snow.
10. (W) If you flush a Mountain Quail, should you look ☐ downhill or ☐ uphill to follow his flight?
11. (W) If you were searching for California Quail at dusk when they are roosting should you look ☐ down on the ground or ☐ up into trees?
12. The Sharp-tailed Grouse is renowned for its ☐ unusually abbreviated courtship ☐ elaborate courtship.
13. Would the Sage Grouse make a better emblem for ☐ a dance hall or ☐ a concert hall?

Birds of Prey

14. An Osprey may dive from as high as ☐ 100 ☐ 200 feet.
15. Does the Red-tailed Hawk tend to perch in a more conspicuous position than the Red-shouldered Hawk? ☐ Yes ☐ No
16. In hunting habits these three hawks, Swainson's, Rough-legged, Ferruginous, most resemble the ☐ Marsh ☐ Red-tailed ☐ Sparrow Hawk.
17. (E) The ☐ Barred Owl ☐ Short-eared Owl has an impressive aerial nuptial flight.
18. The Hawk Owl drops on its prey as does a ☐ Peregrine Falcon ☐ Shrike.
19. The Prairie Falcon ☐ never ☐ often hovers.
20. Which adjective applies best to these species: Broad-winged Hawk, Swainson's Hawk, Rough-legged Hawk? ☐ Aggressive ☐ Inquisitive ☐ Sluggish

43. HABITS—VIREOS AND WARBLERS

Check the appropriate box or boxes and fill in the blank. Each correct answer counts 5.

1. The Blue-winged and Orange-crowned Warblers forage ☐ in the middle level ☐ near the ground.
2. The red-eyed Vireo, when singing, moves about more than does the Solitary. ☐ True ☐ False
3. When not singing, the Solitary Vireo is more sluggish than the Red-eyed. ☐ True ☐ False
4. Woodland picnickers in May would be more likely to see at eye level a ☐ Black-throated Blue Warbler ☐ Black-throated Green Warbler ☐ Black-throated Gray Warbler.
5. (E) An elusive, sweet-voiced minstrel of the swamp is the ☐ Swainson's Warbler ☐ Worm-eating Warbler.
6. (E) In the Texas Delta an elusive warbler of the canopy that sounds like a Parula is almost certainly an_____.
7. (E) Kirtland's, Palm, and Prairie Warblers all ☐ sally after insects ☐ wag their tails.
8. (E) Lovers in apple orchards are likely to be spied on by ☐ Bay-breasted Warbler ☐ Yellow Warblers.
9. (E) Moonshiners in Virginia are more likely to have breeding near their still a ☐ Kentucky Warbler ☐ Tennessee Warbler.
10. (E) On its breeding grounds the ☐ Cape May Warbler ☐ Magnolia Warbler sings from the extreme pinnacle of a spruce or fir.
11. (E) The Blackburnian and Cerulean Warblers are birds of the ☐ middle levels ☐ treetops.
12. (E) The Black-throated Blue Warbler, Myrtle Warbler, and the Ovenbird all ☐ forage at all levels ☐ feign a broken wing to lure intruders from the nest.
13. (E) The Golden-winged Warbler and the Tennessee Warbler in fall feed ☐ from the ground to the treetops ☐ near the ground.
14. (E) The ☐ Hooded Warbler ☐ Wilson's Warbler often fans its tail revealing white tips on its outer feathers.
15. (E) The Pine Warbler often feeds on the ground with ☐ Worm-eating Warblers ☐ Palm Warblers.
16. (E) The ☐ Prothonotary Warbler ☐ Swainson's Warbler sometimes climbs around the trunks of trees.
17. (E) The Tennessee Warbler in spring forages ☐ high ☐ low.
18. (E) The Yellow-throated and Pine Warblers both ☐ creep along the trunk or branches ☐ flutter in front of a leaf.
19. (E) Two warblers chasing each other rapidly through the middle levels of the trees may be ☐ Connecticut Warblers ☐ Worm-eating Warblers ☐ Water thrushes.
20. (W) Which has the most colorful courtship ☐ Grace's Warbler ☐ Lucy's Warbler or ☐ Virginia's Warbler?

44. IDENTIFICATION ON GROUND OR PERCH—
OWLS, WOODPECKERS, FLYCATCHERS

Check the appropriate box or boxes, or fill in the correct words. Each correct answer counts 5.

OWLS

1. Name two owls that often perch on a dune or slight elevation on the ground. 1._____ 2._____
2. Of all our owls, the Long-eared can, for its size, draw itself up into a thinner form than any other. ☐ True ☐ False
3. The Burrowing Owl acts more like a ☐ pompous orator ☐ thief in the night.
4. What owl when perched pumps, and sometimes cocks, its tail?__
   _____

West only

5. The Flammulated Owl perches ☐ near trunk ☐ away from trunk ☐ high up ☐ low down. (Answer two)

WOODPECKERS

6. Name two large species of woodpecker that often perch crosswise on a branch. 1_____ 2._____
7. What woodpecker often perches at a 45 degree angle against the trunk?_____

East only

8. The range of what woodpecker is shown on the map?

FLYCATCHERS

9. The Western Flycatcher quivers its wings when perched. ☐ True ☐ False
10. The Western Wood Pewee does not pump its tail. ☐ True ☐ False
11. The Acadian Flycatcher does not twitch its tail as it sings on a perch. ☐ True ☐ False
12. The ☐ Gray Kingbird ☐ Kiskadee Flycatcher dives after fish as a kingfisher does.
13. The Least Flycatcher jerks its head and tail as it calls. ☐ True ☐ False
14. Say's Phoebe ☐ never ☐ occasionally ☐ often pumps its tail when perched.

44. IDENTIFICATION ON GROUND OR PERCH—
   OWLS, WOODPECKERS, FLYCATCHERS *(Continued)*

Each of these species has a favorite perch. Match the perch and the species.

Species	Perch
15. Olive-sided Flycatcher □	a. Hidden
16. Traill's Flycatcher □	b. Low
17. Western Wood Pewee □	c. Middle height

East only

18. Scissor-tailed Flycatcher □   d. Roadside wire

West only

19. Coues' Flycatcher □   e. Top of low bush

20. Sulphur-bellied Flycatcher □   f. Treetop

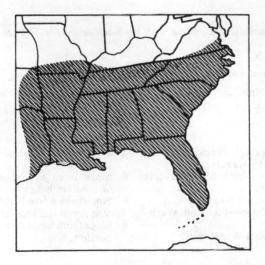

45. IDENTIFICATION ON WATER, GROUND, OR PERCH

Check the appropriate box or fill it in with the right key letter. Each correct answer counts 5.

WATER BIRDS

1. Alcids use their wings when swimming under water. ☐ True ☐ False
2. Is the American Avocet, when feeding, a ☐ diver or a ☐ tilter?
3. Most snipe and sandpipers can swim and dive. ☐ True ☐ False
4. The American Coot swims ☐ "bow high" ☐ "stern high" ☐ with back level.
5. The Black Guillemot, when annoyed, often dabbles nervously in the water with its bill. ☐ True ☐ False
6. The Black-legged Kittiwake can be seen on the surface drinking salt water. ☐ True ☐ False
7. The Clapper Rail and Purple Gallinule, when swimming, bob their heads. ☐ True ☐ False
8. The common Gallinule swims ☐ "bow high" ☐ "stern high" ☐ with back level.
9. The only gull that can dive from the wing and swim under water is a ☐ Kittiwake Gull ☐ Sabine's Gull.
10. The Sora can ☐ swim but not dive ☐ dive but not swim ☐ swim and dive ☐ neither.
11. The Spotted Sandpiper cannot dive from the wing. ☐ True ☐ False

East only

12. The Razorbill Auk swims with its head extended. ☐ True ☐ False

LAND BIRDS

Match habit and species.

13. Water Pipit ☐

14. Wheatear ☐

a. Creeps along branches

b. Nods head as it walks

East only

15. Bachman's, Blackburnian, Cape May Warblers ☐
16. Black-throated Blue, Prairie Warblers ☐
17. Blue-winged Warbler ☐
18. Pine, Yellow-throated Warbler ☐
19. Swainson's Warbler ☐

c. Perches on top of boulder, bobs and bows
d. Sings from an exposed perch of medium height
e. Sing from a low level perch
f. Sing from the tops of trees
g. Sings from top of Northwestern conifer

West only

20. Townsend's Warbler ☐

h. Walks on the ground like an Ovenbird

46. IDENTIFICATION IN FLIGHT—SHOREBIRDS

Check the appropriate box or boxes. Each correct answer counts 5.

1. The flight of the American Golden Plover is swifter and more buoyant than that of the Black-bellied Plover. ☐ True ☐ False
2. The flight of the Lesser Yellowlegs is more buoyant than that of the Greater. ☐ True ☐ False
3. The flight pattern of what curlew most resembles that of the Canada Goose? ☐ Long-billed Curlew ☐ Whimbrel
4. The Killdeer has a spectacular courtship flight. ☐ True ☐ False
5. The Killdeer has never been known to fly at night. ☐ True ☐ False
6. The ☐ Northern Phalarope ☐ Red Phalarope flies like a Sanderling, which it somewhat resembles.
7. The ☐ Red Phalarope ☐ Wilson's Phalarope is noted for often flying in threes, two females apparently chasing one male.
8. (E) The take-off course of the Woodcock resembles ☐ a rocket ☐ the path of a candidate dealing with a ticklish subject.
9. Is the same true of the Common Snipe? ☐ Yes ☐ No
10. What curlew flies high over land in flocks like ducks, or in long lines over the water? ☐ Long-billed Curlew ☐ Whimbrel
11. What sandpiper, if flushed, jumps up suddenly with a harsh *kriek* and hurriedly zigzags away? ☐ Pectoral Sandpiper ☐ Rock Sandpiper
12. What sandpiper seems to fly on the tips of its down-curved wings? ☐ Least Sandpiper ☐ Semipalmated Sandpiper ☐ Spotted Sandpiper
13. What shorebird flies in compact flocks that look yellow in the sun? ☐ Buff-breasted Sandpiper ☐ Eurasian Golden Plover ☐ Surfbird
14. What shorebird, when a flock is flushed, commonly semicircles out over the breakers and lands a little farther up the beach? ☐ Curlew Sandpiper ☐ Sanderling
15. Which, if any, of these species usually raise their wings over their backs when alighting? ☐ American Golden Plover ☐ American Woodcock ☐ Eskimo Curlew ☐ Upland Plover ☐ Willet

East only

16. The Piping Plover sometimes seeks safety by "freezing" as well as by flight. ☐ True ☐ False
17. The wingpits of what plover are silvery white? ☐ American Golden Plover ☐ Mountain Plover
18. What godwit flies in dark, undulating lines? ☐ Hudsonian Godwit ☐ Marbled Godwit
19. When close to a landing, the flight of the ☐ Purple Sandpiper ☐ Sanderling suggests that of the Spotted Sandpiper.

West only

20. The wings of what shorebird, when it jumps into momentary flight to escape a big wave, show a bold black-and-white pattern? ☐ Black Turnstone ☐ Bristle-thighed Curlew ☐ Wandering Tattler

47. IDENTIFICATION IN FLIGHT—GULLS AND TERNS

Match flight description with species by placing key letter in box.
Each correct answer counts 5.

Species

GULLS

1. Black-legged   Kitti-wake ☐
2. Bonaparte's Gull ☐
3. Franklin's Gull ☐
4. Glaucous Gull ☐
5. Glaucous,   Great Black-backed Gulls ☐
6. Herring Gull ☐
7. Mew Gull ☐
8. Ring-billed Gull ☐
9. Sabine's Gull ☐

East only

10. Black-headed Gull ☐
11. Little Gull ☐

TERNS

12. Black Tern ☐
13. Caspian Tern ☐
14. Common Tern ☐
15. Forster's Tern ☐
16. Gull-billed Tern ☐
17. Least Tern ☐

East only

18. Noddy Tern ☐
19. Roseate Tern ☐
20. Sooty Tern ☐

Description

a. A ship follower and soarer, often seen over cities
b. Can capture in air and swallow adult Dovekie
c. Can dive from wing and swim under water
d. Flight buoyant, often in V-shaped flocks
e. Flight graceful, ternlike, with continuous wingbeat; feeds by dipping to the surface, not diving or dropping; breeds Far North
f. Flight like that of Herring Gull, but somewhat more buoyant
g. Flight ternlike with bill pointed down, but seldom dives
h. Flocks sometimes fly in unison like shorebirds
i. In pursuit of insects suggests Black Tern
j. Similar to Bonaparte's Gull but somewhat less buoyant and with slightly less pointed wings
k. Strong, wingbeats slow, soaring flight suggests a Bald Eagle
l. Flocks diving after bait-fish often attract fishermen
m. Has a nighthawklike flight in pursuing insects
n. Has fastest wingbeat of any North American tern
o. Hawks over marshes for insects; wingbeats faster and with more snap than Common Tern's
p. Makes powerful gannetlike dives
q. May fly 200 miles to feed
r. Most graceful flier of coastal terns in spring
s. Seizes prey on wing without getting wet
t. Wingbeats slower than those of *Sterna* terns

48. IDENTIFICATION IN FLIGHT—
OWLS, WOODPECKERS, FLYCATCHERS

Match flight description with species by placing key letter in box.
Each correct answer counts 5.

Description   Species

OWLS

1. Flies with deep wingbeats, buoyantly,   a. Barn Owl
   often reeling, and with legs trailing
   behind ☐
2. Flies with slow flaps of broad,   b. Barred Owl
   rounded wings (northern) ☐
3. Flight falconlike, swift, close to   c. Flammulated Owl
   ground; hunts by day, hovers, drops
   on prey like a shrike ☐
4. If disturbed at nest, flutters on   d. Great Gray Owl
   ground feigning a broken wing ☐
5. In taking off often drops slightly be-   e. Great Horned Owl
   fore flying forward; hunts close to
   ground by night ☐
6. Quarters low over ground like a   f. Hawk Owl
   Marsh Hawk; has an impressive
   daylight aerial courtship flight ☐
7. Sometimes sails on set wings or   g. Long-eared Owl
   soars like a Red-tailed Hawk ☐
8. Strong but jerky flight with upbeat   h. Pygmy Owl
   faster than down (northern) ☐
9. (E) Flies through damp woods with   i. Saw-whet Owl
   buoyant flight and slow wingbeat ☐
10. (W) Forages for moths in open   j. Short-eared Owl
    spaces between tops of ponderosa
    pines ☐
11. (W) Forages in woods by day for   k. Snowy Owl
    lizards, large insects, sometimes
    birds ☐

WOODPECKERS

12. Catches insects in air like a fly-   l. Lewis' Woodpecker
    catcher ☐
13. Drops from a tree almost to the   m. Lewis', Red-cockaded
    ground and then flies low ☐   Woodpeckers
14. In flight suggests a crow; occasion-   n. Pileated Woodpecker
    ally soars ☐
15. (E) Several chase one another amid   o. Red-headed Woodpecker
    upper branches of pines ☐

FLYCATCHERS

16. Quivers its wings in flight ☐   p. Eastern Kingbird

17. Similar to flight of Eastern King-   q. Say's Phoebe
    bird but less fluttering ☐
18. Similar to flight of Eastern Phoebe   r. Scissor-tailed Fly-
    but wingbeats deeper and slower ☐   catcher
19. (E) Has elaborate aerial courtship   s. Western Kingbird
    dance ☐
20. (E) Twitches its tail as it sings ☐   t. Acadian Flycatcher

59

49. IDENTIFICATION IN FLIGHT—LAND BIRDS

Check the box with the appropriate alternative. Each correct answer counts 5.

SWALLOWS

1. The ☐ Bank Swallow ☐ Rough-winged Swallow has a low, somewhat fluttering and mothlike flight.
2. The ☐ Bank Swallow ☐ Rough-winged Swallow often flies repeatedly over the same aerial pathway.
3. The ☐ Cliff Swallow ☐ Violet-green Swallow sometimes flies with White-throated Swifts.
4. The flight of the Rough-winged Swallow is less erratic than that of the Bank Swallow. ☐ True ☐ False
5. The Tree Swallow has less rapid wingbeats than the Barn Swallow. ☐ True ☐ False
6. The Violet-green Swallow has more rapid wingbeats than the Tree Swallow. ☐ True ☐ False

CROWS and JAYS

7. (W) Does the Northwestern Crow ever drop a shellfish on a hard surface to break the shell? ☐ Yes ☐ No
8. Short flights of Clark's Nutcracker are ☐ level ☐ undulating.
9. (E) Steller's Jay has a faster wingbeat than the Blue Jay. ☐ True ☐ False
10. The ☐ Clark's Nutcracker ☐ Piñon Jay plunges down the mountainside and then swoops up with a roar as it spreads its wings.
11. The ☐ Common Crow ☐ Fish Crow often hovers over its food.
12. The Common Crow has slower wingbeats than the Common Raven. ☐ True ☐ False
13. The Common Crow sometimes mobs the ☐ Common Raven ☐ Yellow-billed Magpie.
14. The ☐ Common Raven ☐ Northwestern Crow is given to spectacular aerial evolutions in courtship.
15. The Fish Crow flies with more alternate flapping and sailing than the Common Crow. ☐ True ☐ False
16. The Fish Crow soars more than the Common Crow. ☐True ☐ False
17. The ☐ Green Jay ☐ Mexican Jay, except when breeding, habitually travels in groups of about 20.
18. The ☐ Green Jay ☐ Piñon Jay feeds on the ground in flocks and moves forward by "feathered leapfrog"—that is, those at the back of the flock fly to the front in regular progression.
19. (W) The ☐ Mexican Jay ☐ Scrub Jay often catches insects in the manner of a flycatcher.
20. The ☐ Blue Jay ☐ Gray Jay, of all jays, seems to float most lightly in the air.

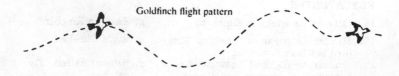

Goldfinch flight pattern

50. BIRD VOICES

Match the species against the voice description by placing the key letter in the right box. Each correct answer counts 5.

Description	Species
1. A loud *quawk*, often heard at dusk ☐	a. American Woodcock
2. A nasal, pleasant *pe-COS, pe-COS* ☐	b. Audubon's Shearwater
3. A ringing song, amazingly loud for so small a bird, seems to go up and down as if on a pogo stick *"see-see-see you-you-you just-look-at-me just-look-at-me"* (Cruickshank) ☐	c. Black-crowned Night Heron
4. A series of harsh *cow cow cow* notes on one pitch, somewhat cuckoolike ☐	d. Black-throated Blue Warbler
5. A slow, wheezy, and burred *chick-a-day-day-day* ☐	e. Boreal Chickadee
6. A whistled *cur-wee;* also a long descending horselike whinny (from a fresh-water marsh) ☐	f. California Quail
7. On breeding grounds a noisy *you're crazy-crazy-crazy* and *cor-RECT, cor-RECT* ☐	g. Gambel's Quail
8. *Yuk yuk yuk*, louder, flatter, slower than flicker's, going up and down irregularly ☐	h. Henslow's Sparrow

GREAT BLUE HERON

BLACK-CROWNED NIGHT HERON

50. BIRD VOICES *(Continued)*

East only

9. A clinking *chap, chap, chapper, chapper, chapper,* a little like knocking pebbles together ☐
10. A hoarse, buzzy, deliberate *B.T.BEEE;* sometimes *zero zero ZEE* ☐
11. A *peent* somewhat like note of Common Nighthawk, but from the ground ☐
12. A short *s'LICK,* often heard at night ☐
13. Croaks and screams *"tell you what, tell you what"* (Chapman) ☐
14. Weird cacklings on breeding grounds, *whither did he go?* (whence local name Wendigo) ☐
15. *Wide-a-wake* ☐

West only

16. A light, high-pitched *tinkle, tinkle, tinkle* ☐
17. A loud *come RIGHT here* ☐
18. A shrill *"meer-meer-meer-meer"* (Pough) winter and summer ☐
19. Call, *ticket, ticket;* rattle thinner and hoarser than in other members of family ☐
20. *Hoo, hoo-hoo, hoooo,* pitch highest in middle ☐

i. Lawrence's Goldfinch

j. Little Blue Heron

k. Marbled Godwit

l. Marbled Murrelet

m. Nuttall's Woodpecker

n. Pied-billed Grebe

o. Pileated Woodpecker

p. Ruby-crowned Kinglet

q. Short-billed Marsh Wren

r. Spotted Owl

s. Sooty Tern

t. Sora

51. NESTS AND EGGS—GENERAL

Certain species of birds have highly characteristic nests and nest sites. Match the descriptions on the right with the species on the left by placing the right key letter in the box. Each correct answer counts 5.

<u>Species</u>

1. Belted Kingfisher ☐

2. Black-billed Magpie ☐

3. Blue-gray Gnatcatcher ☐

4. Brown Creeper ☐

5. Dipper ☐

6. Great Horned Owl ☐

7. Osprey ☐

8. Solitary Sandpiper ☐

9. Verdin ☐

10. White-throated Swift ☐

11. Wood Duck ☐

East only

12. Chimney Swift ☐

13. Ivory-billed Woodpecker ☐

14. Mangrove Cuckoo ☐

15. Rose-throated Becard ☐

16. Smooth-billed Ani ☐

West only

17. Black Swift ☐

18. Cactus Wren ☐

19. Elf Owl ☐

20. Gilded Flicker ☐

<u>Description</u>

a. A ball of thorny twigs near the end of a branch, entrance on the side

b. A bulky communal nest with eggs in layers (in Florida)

c. A cavity with an oval opening (6 x 3 in.) in a large tree in deep woods

d. A chamber at the end of a 4 to 8-foot tunnel in a gravel bank

e. A flat mass of twigs in a dense mangrove

f. A hole in a giant cactus, cotton-wood, or willow

g. A hole in a tree often some distance from water, or a birdbox

h. A huge round mass of sticks with a hole in one side, often in a willow thicket

i. A large mass of sticks in a dead tree, telegraph pole, man-made structure, or on ground

j. A round ball of vegetable fibers hung from near the end of a branch, entrance on the side

k. Cup-shaped, of plant down, bound with spider webs, shingled with lichens

l. Football-shaped, of twigs, thorns, etc., (8 x 18 in.) amid cactus or thorns

m. In a chimney or hollow tree

n. In a crevice in a mountain cliff

o. In a crevice in a moist canyon or sea cliff

p. In a deserted hawk's or crow's nest

q. In a deserted tree nest of a Robin, Cedar Waxwing, or Gray Jay, etc.

r. Often in an old woodpecker hole in a giant cactus

s. Roofed, of mosses, under a waterfall, streambank, or bridge

t. Under a loose hanging slab of bark low on a tree trunk

52. NESTS AND EGGS—FLYCATCHERS

Many species of flycatcher are often hard or impossible to distinguish by appearance, particularly the *Empidonaxes*. But they may often be identified by the kind of nest they build. Significant features are italicized. Match the descriptions on the right with the species on the left by placing the right key letter in the box. Each correct answer counts 5.

Species	Description
Empidonax FLYCATCHER	
1. Dusky Flycatcher ☐	a. Grass-lined cup of plant fibers in *crotch of horizontal limb*, 25 to 60 feet up
2. Traill's Flycatcher ☐	b. Of grass and fiber, *4 to 7 feet up in willows, alders*, etc.
3. Western Flycatcher ☐	c. Of moss, *lined with bark*, from ground to 30 feet up
East only	
4. Acadian Flycatcher ☐	d. Of moss or grasses *on or near ground* near water, in forest
5. Least Flycatcher ☐	e. Of plant fibers and grasses, *in upright fork of tree*, 8 to 40 feet high
6. Yellow-bellied Flycatcher ☐	f. Of plant fibers tied by cobwebs to a branch against a trunk, *usually under another branch*
West only	
7. Buff-breasted Flycatcher ☐	g. Of rootlets, etc., *swung like a hammock* between twigs near end of branch, 4 to 20 feet up, often over water, with long untidy wisps of vegetation hanging from bottom or sides
8. Gray Flycatcher	h. Of shreds and grasses, *in crotch of shrub 2 to 4 feet up*
9. Hammond's Flycatcher ☐	i. *Loose, bulky*, of bark fibers lined with feathers, *low in a bush*
OTHER FLYCATCHERS	
10. Beardless Flycatcher ☐	j. *Ball of plant fibers* with plant down in center, entrance on side, in tree or shrub, any height
11. Eastern Kingbird ☐	k. Large, deep, *lined with yellow grasses* and usually without lichens
12. Olive-sided Flycatcher ☐	l. Of coarse twigs, lined with grass, flimsy, *in thicket of red mangrove*, often over salt water

52. NESTS AND EGGS—FLYCATCHERS *(Continued)*

13. Say's Phoebe ☐   m. Of hair, fur, feathers, and snakeskin in a deserted woodpecker *hole in a giant cactus*

14. Western Wood Pewee ☐   n. Of mud and grass on ledges *below bridge*, building, or cliff, near water

15. Wied's Crested Flycatcher ☐   o. Of mud and moss, often *under a bridge* or eaves, or on some other man-made structure, in a cave or on a little cliff, near water

East only

16. Eastern Phoebe ☐   p. Of mud and some moss, often wool-lined, in cave, *abandoned well*, *mine-shaft*, or other man-made structure

17. Eastern Wood Pewee ☐   q. Of trash, in cavity, 5 to 60 feet high, *often with snakeskin*

18. Gray Kingbird ☐   r. Of twigs and grasses, bulky, ragged without, neat within, 3 to 20 feet up in bush, tree, stump, or structure, often near water

19. Great Crested Flycatcher ☐   s. Of twigs, 10 to 50 feet up in *crotch of horizontal branch of conifer*

20. The range of what landbird (not a flycatcher) whose winter range was only recently discovered is shown on these maps?

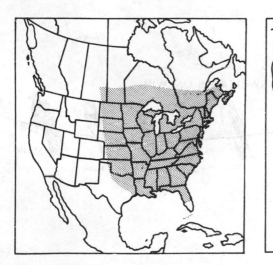

Significant features are italicized. Match descriptions with species names by placing right key letter in box. Each correct answer counts 5.

<u>Species</u>   <u>Description</u>

SWALLOWS

1. Bank Swallow ☐

2. Barn Swallow ☐

3. Cliff Swallow ☐

4. Purple Martin ☐

5. Rough-winged Swallow ☐

6. Violet-green Swallow ☐

WRENS

7. Canyon Wren ☐

8. House Wren ☐

9. Long-billed Marsh Wren ☐

10. Rock Wren ☐

11. Winter Wren ☐

a. *A burrow* in a sandbank, in colonies

b. *A hole in a tree*, or a nesting box

c. In an avian *apartment house* of 8 to 32 rooms

d. *Inside a barn*, on a rafter or against a beam; sometimes under a bridge

e. Of mud, gourd-shaped, on *outside of barn* or other building, or face of cliff

f. *Crevices in walls* and caves, under bridges, sometimes burrows

g. A ball of grass with a side entrance, attached to reeds or bushes in a marsh

h. In root mass of fallen tree, or in other tangle near ground

i. *Of twigs, in any cavity* or birdbox

j. Of twigs, moss, etc., *in cavity in rocks*, also in buildings

k. With a *little stone pathway* leading to it

SWALLOWS ON WIRE

Violet-green   Barn   Cliff   Tree   Rough-winged   Bank   Martin

WARBLERS

East only

12. Black-throated Green Warbler ☐

13. Cape May Warbler ☐

14. Cerulean Warbler ☐

15. Connecticut Warbler ☐

16. Kirtland's Warbler ☐

17. Louisiana Waterthrush ☐

18. Ovenbird ☐

19. Prothonotary Warbler ☐

20. Yellow Warbler ☐

l. *Arched*, and with side entrance, bulky, of grass and leaves, concealed, on forest floor

m. Bulky, of leaves and grass, hidden in *cavity in streambank*

n. Cup-shaped, of *silver-gray plant fibers* in fork of low bush or sapling

o. Cup-shaped, of twigs, birchbark, bound with spider webs, *on limb of conifer* 15 to 70 feet up

p. *In woodpecker hole*, cavity, or birdbox, near water

q. Large for a warbler, of sphagnum moss, in end clump of vegetation, *near top of spruce or fir*, 30 to 60 feet up

r. Of bark and vegetable fibers, on ground in *groves of jack pines*

s. Of grasses, in moss, on ground *in tamarack swamp*

t. Shallow, cup-shaped of grasses bound with spider webs, decorated with lichens, *suspended in fork of branch*, 20 to 90 feet up

KINGBIRD TAILS

EASTERN

WESTERN

CASSIN'S

54. IDENTIFICATION BY RANGE AND SEASON—
LAND BIRDS

Check the appropriate box. Each correct answer counts 5.

1. (E) A big, black bird near the mouth of the Rio Grande is almost certainly a ☐ Common Raven ☐ White-necked Raven ☐ Fish Crow.
2. A big, black bird on the shores of Hudson Bay is almost certainly a ☐ Common Crow ☐ Common Raven.
3. A bird artist in Taos, New Mexico, might expect to see a ☐ Black-billed Cuckoo ☐ Yellow-billed Cuckoo.
4. A bird watcher reports a winter vireo from North Carolina. Is it a ☐ Red-eyed Vireo or a ☐ Solitary Vireo?
5. A housewife in Maine reports a ☐ Ruby-throated Hummingbird ☐ Rufous Hummingbird at her hummingbird feeder.
6. An apple grower in Ontario had a ☐ Cassin's Kingbird ☐ Eastern Kingbird ☐ Western Kingbird in his orchard.
7. A bird watcher from the East on a trip to Montana saw several ☐ Red-shafted Flickers ☐ Yellow-shafted Flickers. ☐ Probably saw both species.
8. A swift flying over Chicago is a ☐ Chimney Swift ☐ Vaux's Swift.
9. Audubon Christmas census takers on Long Island sometimes report a ☐ Hermit Thrush ☐ Swainson's Thrush.
10. Motoring through Kansas in summer you might see an ☐ Eastern Bluebird ☐ Mountain Bluebird ☐ Western Bluebird on the roadside wire.
11. On a summer trip through the Minnesota countryside you see a longspur. Is it a ☐ McCown's Longspur or a ☐ Chestnut-collared Longspur?
12. (E) The black-throated Warbler ☐ Blue Warbler ☐ Gray Warbler ☐ Green Warbler breeds in Saskatchewan.
13. The chickadee that Theodore Roosevelt observed on his tramps through Rock Creek Park in Washington, D.C., was the ☐ Black-capped Chickadee ☐ Carolina Chickadee.
14. The correct name of the crested jay of the Rockies is the ☐ Blue Jay ☐ Scrub Jay ☐ Steller's Jay.
15. The early March swallow along the Middle Atlantic coast is the ☐ Bank Swallow ☐ Tree Swallow.
16. The late George Apley probably fed a ☐ Black-capped Chickadee ☐ Boreal Chickadee at his bird feeder in Boston.
17. The only *Empidonax* in Alabama in summer is the ☐ Acadian Flycatcher ☐ Traill's Flycatcher.
18. The only brown-backed swallow in southern Mississippi in summer is the ☐ Bank Swallow ☐ Rough-winged Swallow ☐ young Tree Swallow.
19. The only *Empidonax* in northern Newfoundland in summer is the ☐ Traill's Flycatcher ☐ Yellow-bellied Flycatcher.
20. The summer waxwing of North Dakota is the ☐ Bohemian Waxwing ☐ Cedar Waxwing.

55. *SIC PERPETUAT MEMORIA*

The names of many birds commemorate famous ornithologists or other persons. Some 60 individuals have achieved such immortality in the names of North American birds; 40 of the better-known birds or persons are included in this quiz. Match the species with the person by placing the right key letter in the box. Each correct answer counts 2 1/2.

Person	Species
1. Audubon's ☐	a. Auklet, Finch, Kingbird, Sparrow
2. Baird's ☐	b. Blackbird, Sparrow
3. Barrow's ☐	c. Bunting
4. Bewick's ☐	d. Cormorant
5. Bonaparte's ☐	e. Eider, Jay
6. Brewer's ☐	f. Flycatcher
7. Bullock's ☐	g. Flycatcher
8. Cassin's ☐	h. Goldeneye
9. Clark's ☐	i. Goose, Gull
10. Cooper's ☐	j. Gull
11. Forster's ☐	k. Gull
12. Gambel's ☐	l. Hawk
13. Harris' ☐	m. Hawk, Sparrow
14. Leach's ☐	n. Hawk, Thrush, Warbler
15. Le Conte's ☐	o. Hummingbird
16. Lewis' ☐	p. Longspur
17. Lincoln's ☐	q. Murrelet
18. Ross' ☐	r. Nutcracker
19. Say's ☐	s. Oriole
20. Smith's ☐ (map on left below)	t. Petrel
21. Sprague's ☐ (map on right below)	u. Petrel, Phalarope, Plover, Warbler

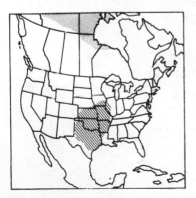 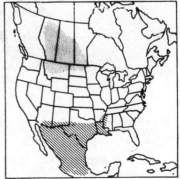

55. *SIC PERPETUAT MEMORIA (Continued)*

22. Steller's ☐

23. Swainson's ☐

24. Traill's ☐

25. Wilson's ☐

East only

26. Bachman's ☐

27. Cory's ☐

28. Henslow's ☐

29. Kirtland's ☐

West only

30. Abert's ☐

31. Allen's ☐

32. Bendier's ☐

33. Brandt's ☐

34. Hammond's ☐

35. Heermann's ☐

36. Hutton's ☐

37. Kittlitz's ☐

38. McKay's ☐

39. Nuttall's ☐

40. Vaux's ☐

v. Phoebe

w. Pipit

x. Quail

y. Sandpiper, Sparrow

z. Shearwater

aa. Sparrow

bb. Sparrow

cc. Sparrow, Thrasher

dd. Sparrow

ee. Swift

ff. Tern

gg. Thrasher

hh. Towhee

ii. Vireo

jj. Warbler, Shearwater

kk. Warbler

ll. Woodpecker

mm. Woodpecker

nn. Wren

TOWNSEND'S SOLITAIRE

56. GENUS NAMES—SHORT OR EASY

In studying birds' names many bird watchers take an interest in learning the birds' scientific names. Without making a great effort many bird watchers pick up a number of those more frequently used or those of common birds. Some scientific names bear a close resemblance to the English names. For figuring out others, some knowledge of Greek or Latin is helpful. The present quiz contains the shortest and easiest genus names of those species that occur annually in North America. Match the English name with the genus name by putting the right key letter in the box. Each correct answer counts 2 1/2.

Genus name	English name
1. Aix ☐	a. Anhinga
2. Anas ☐	b. Barn Owl
3. Anhinga (E) ☐	c. Barred Owl
4. Anser ☐	d. Brant
5. Aquila ☐	e. Chickadees and some other titmice
6. Ardea ☐	f. Common Gallinule
7. Asio ☐	g. Cranes
8. Branta ☐	h. Crows, Ravens
9. Bubo ☐	i. Fulmar
10. Buteo ☐ (range map of one	j. Golden Eagle
11. Chen ☐ species on left below)	k. Great Blue Heron
12. Circus ☐	l. Great Horned Owl
13. Columba ☐	m. Gulls, most
14. Corvus ☐	n. Mute Swan
15. Cygnus (E) ☐ (range map on right below)	o. House Sparrow

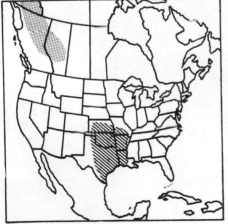 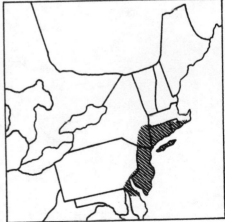

56. GENUS NAMES—SHORT OR EASY *(Continued)*

16. Fulmarus ☐

17. Gallinula ☐

18. Grus ☐

19. Junco ☐

20. Larus ☐

21. Mergus ☐

22. Mimus ☐

23. Olor ☐

24. Otus ☐

25. Parus ☐

26. Passer ☐

27. Pelecanus ☐

28. Phalaropus ☐

29. Pica ☐

30. Rallus ☐

31. Sitta ☐

32. Spinus ☐

33. Sterna ☐

34. Strix ☐

35. Sturnus ☐

36. Turdus ☐

37. Tyto ☐

38. Uria ☐

39. Vireo ☐

40. Xema ☐

p. Juncos

q. Long-eared Owl and certain other owls

r. Magpies

s. Mallard and certain other ducks

t. Marsh Hawk

u. Mergansers, most

v. Mockingbird

w. Murres

x. Nuthatches

y. Pelicans

z. Pine Siskin

aa. Rails

bb. Red Phalarope

cc. Harlan's Hawk, etc.

dd. Robin

ee. Rock Dove

ff. Sabine's Gull

gg. Screech Owl

hh. Snow Goose, etc.

ii. Starling

jj. Terns, most

kk. Vireos

ll. Whistling Swan

mm. White-fronted Goose

nn. Wood Duck

FOR THE SPECIALIST

LAPLAND

SMITH'S

LONGSPUR TAILS

MCCOWN'S

CHESTNUT-COLLARED

57. RIDDLES—BIRDS AND NOUNS

Fill in the blank with the appropriate bird name. Each correct name counts 5.

1. A dunce. _____
2. A gurgitation. _____
3. A ladle. _____
4. Disease of horses' hoofs. _____
5. Gauge of craziness. _____
6. Gay cloth for decorations. _____
7. Girl with red hair. _____
8. (W) Gold coin of Chile, Colombia, Ecuador. _____
9. Gone with the wind. _____
10. (E) Hat (slang). _____
11. Instrument for opening nuts. _____
12. Jack's mother. _____
13. Light piece of ordnance (15th-17th century). _____
14. Mechanism for lifting. _____
15. One easily cheated. _____
16. Prince of the Church. _____
17. Split by Lincoln. _____
18. (W) Talebearer. _____
19. Ten dollars. _____
20. Bar with which Archimedes might have raised the earth. _____

58. RIDDLES—BIRDS AND VERBS

Fill in the blank with the appropriate bird name. Each correct na counts 5.

1. To appear to touch water without actually doing so. _____
2. To bend low to avoid a blow. _____
3. To complain. _____
4. To defraud (slang). _____
5. To dupe. _____
6. To elongate, as the neck. _____
7. To engage in frolicsome sport. _____
8. To flinch. _____
9. To fly about looking for prey. _____
10. To hunt venison. _____
11. To imitate without understanding. _____
12. To lead a suit that one's partner can trump. _____
13. To boast. _____
14. To protest. _____
15. To raise checks (slang). _____
16. To scintillate rapidly. _____
17. To shoot at. _____
18. To take through the gullet. _____
19. To talk in a familiar manner. _____
20. To tie tightly. _____

59. BIRDS IN THE BIBLE

Fill in the blank with the appropriate bird name. Each correct *name* counts 5.

1. "But the_____found no rest for the sole of her foot." Genesis 8:9

2. "And it came to pass, that at even the_____came up, and covered the camp." (They served as food for the children of Israel in the Wilderness.) Exodus 16:13

3. "For the king of Israel is come out to seek a flea, as when one doth hunt a_____in the mountains." I Samuel 26:20

4. "Once in three years came the navy of Tharshish, bringing gold, and silver, ivory, and apes, and_____." I Kings 10:22

5. "And the_____brought him bread and flesh in the morning, and bread and flesh in the evening; and he drank of the brook." I Kings 17:6

6. "Gavest thou the goodly wings unto the peacocks? or wings and feathers unto the_____." Job 39:13

7. "Doth the_____fly by thy wisdom, and stretch her wings toward the south?" Job 39:26

8. "Yea, the_____hath found an house, and the_____a nest for herself, where she may lay her young, even thine altars, O Lord of hosts, my King, and my God." Psalm 84:3-4

9. "I am like a_____of the wilderness: I am like an_____of the desert." Psalm 102:6-7

10. "The way of an_____in the air." Proverbs 30:19

11. "And the voice of the_____is heard in our land." Song of Solomon 2:12

12. "Yea, the_____in the heaven knoweth her appointed times; and the turtle and the_____and the swallow observe the time of their coming." Jeremiah 8:7

13. "Be ye therefore wise as serpents and harmless as_____." Matthew 10:16

14. "Are not two_____sold for a farthing?" Matthew 10:29

15. "As a_____gathereth her_____under her wings." Matthew 23:37

16. "Jesus said unto him, Verily I say unto thee, That this night, before the_____crow, thou shalt deny me thrice." Matthew 26:34

a. Chickens.
b. Cock.
c. Crane.
d. Dove.
e. Doves.
f. Eagle.
g. Hawk.
h. Hen.
i. Ostrich.
j. Owl.
k. Partridge.
l. Peacocks.
m. Pelican.
n. Quails.
o. Ravens.
p. Sparrow.
q. Sparrows.
r. Stork.
s. Swallow.
t. Turtle (dove)

60. PHILATELY—NEW WORLD, BRITISH COMMONWEALTH, SOUTHWEST AFRICA*

These species are illustrated on the stamps of the countries listed on the right. Match the country with the bird-bearing stamp(s) by placing the right letter in the box. Each correct answer counts 5.

Birds on Stamps

1. Araucanian Dove, 1948, 60¢ ☐
2. Argus Pheasant, 1893=1897 5¢ ☐
3. Black-necked Swan (1p), Upland Goose (4p), Gentoo Penguin (2sh6p), 1938=1946 ☐
4. Black Swan, 1854=1912 ☐
5. Brush-tongued Lory, 1897, 2sh6p ☐
6. Brush Turkey, 1939=1943, 2sh6p ☐ 2sh6p ☐
7. Middle American Jacana (12¢, 2p) Gundlach Hawk (14¢), Ivory-billed Woodpecker (5p), AP, 1956 ☐
8. Fire-crowned Bishop (6p), Giant Plantain Eater (2sh6p), 1959 ☐
9. Rockhopper Penguin (1½p), Molly-mauk (2½p) Flightless Rail (5sh), 1954=1958 ☐
10. Great Bustard, 1935, ½p ☐
11. Kandavu Parrot, 1959, 4sh ☐
12. Kavirondo Crane, 1935=1938, 1¢ ☐
13. Kookaburra, 1913=1943, 6p ☐
14. Loon, 1957, 5¢ ☐
15. Notornis, 1956, 8p ☐
16. Peacock, 1938, 1r, 2r; 1931, 2½a ☐
17. Quetzal, 1879=1954 ☐ ☐
18. Sooty Tern, 1934, 1sh ☐
19. Terutero, 1923, 5m=2p ☐
20. Whooping Crane, 1957, 3¢ ☐

Country

a. Ascension
b. Australia
c. British Solomon Islands
d. Burma, Jaipur
e. Canada
f. Chile
g. Cuba
h. Falkland Islands
i. Fiji
j. Ghana
k. Guatemala
l. Kenya, Uganda
m. Labuan, North Borneo
n. New Zealand
o. Southwest Africa
p. Tonga
q. Tristan da Cunha
r. United States of America
s. Uruguay
t. Western Australia

*Source for philately quizzes: *Scott's Stamp Catalogue* (Standard Postage Stamp Catalogue, 1961 Combined Edition, Scott Publications, Inc., New York, 1961).

61. PHILATELY—OLD WORLD—I

Birds on Stamps

Country

1. African Marabou, Ethiopian Ibis, Red Pelican, Senegalese Jabiru, Stork, White Egret, 1959, 5c-2s ☐
2. Albatross, Cormorant, Sea Swallow, Sea Gull, 1955, 200fr-1000fr ☐
3. Albatross, Emperor Penguin, 1956 =1959, 50fr-200fr ☐
4. Bataieur Eagle, 1938, 1 lire, 5 lire ☐
5. Bearded Eagle, Pelican, 1954, 25d, 30d. ☐
6. Beth Shearim Eagle, Marisa Eagle, 1950, 30p, 100p. ☐
7. Bird from antique mosaic in Museum of Sousse, 1949, AP 200fr. ☐
8. Black Cock, Black Stork, Cormorant, Hawk, Hoopoe, Owl, 1959, 5pf =40pf. ☐
9. Black-headed Gull, Buzzard, Grouse, Lammergeier, Peregrine Falcon, Eagle, 1934=1939, 10rp=2f. ☐
10. Bullfinch, Goldfinch, Golden Oriole, Kingfisher, Nuthatch, Titmouse, Woodpecker, 1959, 20h-1. 20k. ☐
11. Common Heron, Cormorant, Crested Heron, Curlew, Great Egret, Little Egret, Purple Heron, Spoonbill, 1959, 10f-3fo. ☐
12. Cormorant Fishing, Mandarin Duck, Pheasant, 1953=1955, 3y,5y, 100y. ☐
13. Crown Pigeon, 1959, 7c,12c,17c. ☐
14. Curlew, Gray Wagtail, Lapwing, Pelican, Spoonbill, Stilt, White Heron, 1957=1959, 5b-5leu. ☐
15. Eagle, Gonolek, Merle Amethyste, 1960, 100fr-500fr. ☐
16. Eagle, Ostrich, Royal Heron, Sparrow Hawk, Sea Gull, 1957=1958, 15c-10p. ☐
17. Eagle over Mountain Pass, 1929, 20c. ☐
18. Eagle, double-headed, with inscription SHQIPENIA 1913=1920 ☐
19. Eider Ducks, Falcon, 1959=1960, 90a,25k. ☐
20. Elate Hornbill, Fishing Vulture, Great White Egret, Jacana, Pepper Bird, Plantain-eater, Weaver, 1960=1953, 1¢-12¢. ☐

a. Albania
b. Andorra
c. Czechoslovakia
d. Dutch New Guinea
e. French Southern and Antarctic Territories
f. German Democratic Republic
g. Hungary
h. Iceland
i. Israel
j. Italian East Africa
k. Japan
l. Liberia
m. Liechtenstein
n. Mali
o. Monaco
p. Romania
q. Somalia
r. Spanish Sahara
s. Tunisia
t. Yugoslavia

62. PHILATELY—OLD WORLD—II

Birds on Stamps	Country

1. Flying Swans, 1956, 30ö-60ö. ☐   a. Algeria

2. Gallic Cock, 1944, 10¢-50¢. ☐   b. Angola

3. Great Titmouse, 1952, 10m+2m—25m+   c. Austria
   5m. ☐

4. Kagu, 1905=1948. ☐   d. China

5. Long-tailed Fowl of Tosa, 1951 5y. ☐   e. Belgian Congo

6. Marabou Storks and Vultures, 1939, 1fr+   f. Denmark
   1fr—4.50fr+4.50fr.

7. *Melierax mechowi, Merops apiaster*, etc.,   g. Ethiopia
   1951, 5¢-50a. ☐

8. Moroccan Shag, 1952, 5c+5c—60c+15c. ☐   h. Finland

9. Night Herons over Mt. Sanin, 1946, 12.50   i. France
   pi. ☐

10. Ostrich, SP, 10¢-10 lire+2.50 lire. ☐   j. French Equatorial
        Africa

11. Shearwater over Moorea landscape; also   k. French Polynesia
    over Maupiti shoreline, 1948, AP, 50fr,
    200fr. ☐

12. Snake Birds, 1953, 500fr. ☐   l. Ifni

13. Somali Ostriches, 1919, 12g. ☐   m. Japan

14. "Storks" by Chelmonski, 1959, 40g. ☐   n. Lebanon

15. Storks over Mosque, 1949, 50fr-200fr. ☐   o. Libia

16. "The Rooks Have Arrived" by A. K. Savra-   p. Madagascar
    sov, 1956, 40k. ☐

17. Uratelornis, 1954, 8fr,15fr. ☐   q. New Caledonia

18. "White-shouldered" (Imperial) Eagle,   r. Poland
    1925, 20g-80g. ☐

19. White-thighed Hornbill, 1952, 5c+5c—60c+   s. Spanish Guinea
    15c. ☐

20. Wild Goose, 1897=1898, $1-$5. ☐   t. Union of Soviet
        Socialist Republics

63. CROSSWORD-PUZZLE BIRD NAMES—I

Fill in the missing letters. Each correct answer counts 2 1/2.

1. A communal nester   -N-
2. Audubon's   ---A---A
3. Baltimore's bird   --I--E
4. Biblical eagle   G---
5. Brazilian macaw   -R---
6. Butcherbird   S----E
7. Canary's ancestor   --R--
8. Carolina rail   --R-
9. Clapper's genus   --L---
10. Dove (Lat.)   ----MB-
11. Downy duck   ---E-
12. Eagle on U.S. coat of arms   -A--
13. European kite   ---D-
14. Expert diving duck   ---W
15. Extinct New Zealand bird   --A
16. Great Horned Owl's genus   -U--
17. High seas harrier   J--G--
18. Long-eared Owl's genus   -S--
19. Macaw   --A
20. Mother Carey's chicken   ---R--
21. Muscovy duck   P---
22. Nile wader   -B--
23. Ostrich cousin   -H--
24. Poe's croaker   --V--
25. Rhymes with Congo (Aus.)   ----G-
26. Said to fly straight   --O-
27. Said to have eaten elephants   --C
28. Scarlet songbird   -A-A---
29. Sea eagle   -R-
30. Sea swallow   --R-
31. South African finch   ---K
32. Snowbird   ---C-
33. Spoonbill's genus   -J---
34. The great one has gone   -U-
35. Trumpeter's genus   --O-
36. U.S. Colonel's insignia   --G--
37. Water turkey   -N---G-
38. White-fronted Goose's genus   ----R
39. Young turkey   -O---
40. Zoo attraction   -M-

64. CROSSWORD-PUZZLE BIRD NAMES—II

Fill in the missing letters. Each correct answer counts 2 1/2.

1.	Adjutant	M---B--
2.	African bustard	K---
3.	Apteryx	---I
4.	A talker	-Y---
5.	A trogonid	--O-O-
6.	Australian and New Zealand rail	P---K-
7.	Australian harrier	--H-
8.	Baker bird	----E-O
9.	Bustard genus	--I-
10.	Buzzard	---E-
11.	Chaffinch	----K
12.	Corn crake genus	---X
13.	Crane genus	G---
14.	Dovekie	--T---
15.	Forest parrot, N.Z.	--K-
16.	Gadwall's genus	---S
17.	Great spotted kiwi	R----A
18.	Gunner's broadbill	---U-
19.	Indian thrush	-H---
20.	Long-billed cockatoo (Aus.)	C---L--
21.	Long-legged wader	-V----
22.	Large domestic mallard	---E-
23.	Male has curved bill (N.Z.)	H---
24.	Mauritius' most famous dead	---O
25.	Monkey-face's genus	-Y--
26.	Native companion (Aus.)	B---G-
27.	New Zealand mutton-bird	-I
28.	New Zealand wood hen	W---
29.	Once the gourmet's bunting	--T---N
30.	Oriental cuckoo	K---
31.	Persian "nightingale"	--L--L
32.	Plume-bearer	-G---
33.	Redhead's genus	-Y--Y-
34.	Sabine Gull's genus	X---
35.	Sheep-killing parrot	--A
36.	Stake-driver	--T---N
37.	Tropical flycatching bird	J---M--
38.	Walks under water	--Z--
39.	West Indian endemic	---Y
40.	Wood duck genus	-I-

Fill in the missing letters. Each correct answer counts 2 1/2.

1. Affectionate N.Z. parrot — K---P-
2. Australian parrot — -O--L--
3. Black-necked Stork (Aus.) — --B-R-
4. Boobook Owl (Aus.) — M-P---
5. 80,000 made king's cloak (Hawaii) — O-
6. Finchlike Hawaiian bird — P-L---
7. Great Black-backed Gull's genus — ---U-
8. Green with parrotlike bill (Hawaii) — -U
9. Hawaiian Goose — -E--
10. Honey Buzzard — --R-
11. Hummingbird — -O--B--
12. Indian buzzard — --S-
13. Indian hawk — -H-K--
14. Red-throated Loon's genus — --V--
15. Lyrebird genus — M---R-
16. Magpie — ---
17. Magpie genus — --C-
18. Mallee fowl — GN--
19. Marabou — -R--L-
20. Megapode — M----
21. Mr. Headdown's genus — ---T-
22. Mocker genus — -I---
23. Mousebird — --L-
24. Near-flightless bird of New Caledonia — ---U
25. Noddy Tern (Hawaii) — --I-
26. No keel on sternum — --T-T-
27. Notornis, N.Z. — T-K---
28. Orange honey creeper (Hawaii) — -K---
29. Painted Bunting (Creole) — -A--
30. Parson bird — T--
31. Pied Oystercatcher (Aus.) — S----E
32. Rose-breasted Cockatoo — G----
33. Royal cloak-maker, extinct (Hawaii) — ---O
34. Samoa's barn owl — L---
35. Sand Partridge — --E--E
36. Scarlet with black wings (Hawaii) — -P-P---
37. Short-billed gull — --W
38. Vermilion with pink sickle-bill (Hawaii) — I---
39. Walks on lily pads — J---N-
40. Whale-bird — ----N

66. NAMES OF YESTERYEAR

Many of these names were used by Wilson, Audubon, and other early naturalists. To us today they have the flavor of Chippendale and old lace. Match the 1957 *A.O.U. Check-list* names with the old-time names by placing the right letter in the box. Each correct answer counts 2 1/2.

Old-time Name

1. Bartram's Sandpiper ☐
2. Bay-winged Bunting ☐
3. Beach Oxeye ☐
4. Black-throated Bunting ☐
5. Buffalo-headed Duck ☐
6. Butcher-bird ☐
7. Carolina Pigeon ☐
8. Carrion Crow ☐
9. Chewink ☐
10. Clark's Crow ☐
11. Cock-of-the-Plains ☐
12. Golden-crested Wren ☐
13. Golden-winged Woodpecker ☐
14. Great-footed Hawk ☐
15. Ground Robin ☐
16. Louisiana Tanager ☐
17. Meadow Oxeye ☐
18. Nonpareil ☐
19. Purre ☐
20. Reed-bird ☐
21. Rice Bunting ☐
22. Ruby-crested Wren ☐
23. Shore Lark ☐
24. Snowflake ☐
25. Summer Duck ☐
26. Summer Red-bird ☐
27. Summer Yellow-bird ☐
28. Titlark ☐
29. Turtle Dove ☐
30. White-bellied Swallow ☐
31. White-headed Eagle ☐
32. Yellow-rumped Warbler ☐

1957 Check-list Name

a. Acadian Flycatcher
b. Bald Eagle
c. Black Vulture
d. Blue-winged Warbler
e. Bobolink
f. Bobolink
g. Bufflehead
h. Clark's Nutcracker
i. Dickcissel
j. Dunlin
k. Golden-crowned Kinglet
l. Greater Prairie Chicken
m. Horned Lark
n. Labrador Duck
o. Limpkin
p. Least Sandpiper
q. Mourning Dove
r. Mourning Dove
s. Myrtle Warbler
t. Ovenbird
u. Painted Bunting
v. Peregrine Falcon
w. Pine Warbler
x. Ruby-crowned Kinglet
y. Rufous-sided Towhee
z. Rufous-sided Towhee
aa. Sage Grouse
bb. Semipalmated Sandpiper
cc. Shrike
dd. Snow Bunting
ee. Summer Tanager
ff. Tree Swallow

East only

33. Blue-winged Yellow Warbler ☐
34. Golden-crowned Thrush ☐
35. Green-crested Flycatcher ☐
36. Pied Duck ☐
37. Pine-creeping Warbler ☐
38. Pinnated Grouse ☐
39. Scolopaceous Courlan ☐
40. Wood Robin ☐

gg. Upland Plover
hh. Vesper Sparrow
ii. Water Pipit
jj. Western Tanager
kk. Wood Duck
ll. Wood Thrush
mm. Yellow-shafted Flicker
nn. Yellow Warbler

67. NAMES OF YESTERDAY

The following English names are not to be found in the 1957 *A.O.U.*
Check-list. What are these birds' names now? Each correct answer
counts 5.

Present Species Name

1. Alder Flycatcher
2. American Three-toed Woodpecker
3. Arctic Three-toed Woodpecker
4. Arkansas Kingbird
5. Brünnich's Murre
6. Cabot's Tern (E)
7. Derby Flycatcher (E)
8. Duck Hawk
9. European Teal
10. Florida Gallinule
11. Holbœll's Grebe
12. Hudsonian Curlew
13. Hungarian Partridge
14. Olive-backed Thrush
15. Red-backed Sandpiper
16. Richardson's Owl
17. Texas Nighthawk
18. Texas Sparrow (E)
19. Wilson's Snipe
20. Wright's Flycatcher

Sanderling before waves

68. WHERE, OH WHERE HAS THE BRONZED GRACKLE GONE?

The 1957 *A.O.U. Check-list* no longer gives English names to subspecies as it did previously. The following former names of subspecies are not in the 1957 *Check-list*. Under what species names are they now included? Each correct answer counts 5.

Present Species Name

1. Mearns's Quail _____

East only

2. Acadian Chickadee _____
3. Audubon's Oriole _____
4. Bicknell's Thrush _____
5. Bronzed Grackle _____

West only

6. Beal's Petrel _____
7. Bell's Sparrow _____
8. Brewster's Egret _____
9. Cackling Goose _____
10. Calaveras Warbler _____
11. California Jay _____
12. Chestnut-backed Bluebird _____
13. Lead-colored Bush-Tit _____
14. Lutescent Warbler _____
15. Natalie's Sapsucker _____
16. Peale's Falcon _____
17. Pileolated Warbler _____
18. Plumbeous Gnatcatcher _____
19. Spurred Towhee _____
20. Treganza's Heron _____

69. FALCONRY

The sport of falconry, of ancient Oriental origin, was much pursued by royalty and the nobility in medieval Europe. It involved the taming and flying of falcons and other hawks after game. A specialized vocabulary arose, of which the following were some of the more common words and phrases. Match the definition with the word by placing the right letter in the box. Each correct answer counts 5.

Word	Definition
1. Cadge ☐	a. A bunch of feathers attached to a long cord, often baited with meat
2. Cast ☐	b. A cage or building for hawks
3. Eyas ☐	c. Falcon's nest
4. Eyrie ☐	d. Female bird
5. Falcon ☐	e. Grown hawk caught in the wild
6. Haggard ☐	f. Gyrfalcon and Peregrine Falcon
7. Jesses ☐	g. Male bird
8. Lure ☐	h. Prey
9. Mews ☐	i. Rings attaching bells to jesses
10. Noble falcons ☐	j. Square frame on which hawks were carried to the field
11. Quarry ☐	k. Straps around the hawk's legs
12. Tiercel ☐	l. To get above fleeing quarry
13. To imp ☐	m. To hover above the master
14. To man a hawk ☐	n. To mend a feather
15. To mew ☐	o. To moult
16. To seel ☐	p. To plunge after prey
17. To stoop ☐	q. To sew a hawk's eyes closed with a fine thread through the lids
18. To take the air ☐	r. To tame a hawk
19. To wait on ☐	s. Two hawks
20. Varvels ☐	t. Young falcon reared from the nest

70. WHEN IS A FLOCK NOT A FLOCK?

When it is a flight of doves, or when it is:

1. A bevy of _____
2. A charm of _____
3. A company of _____
4. A congregation, or a building, of _____
5. A covert of _____
6. A covey of _____
7. A dropping of _____
8. An exaltation of _____
9. A fall of _____
10. A gaggle, or a skein, of _____
11. A muster of _____
12. A nide of _____
13. A raft, or a plump, of _____
14. A siege of _____
15. A sord of _____
16. A spring of _____
17. A stand, or a wing, of _____
18. A watch of _____
19. A whiteness of _____
20. A wisp of _____

Some of these go back to A.D. 1486, or before, in literature and in hunting usages. Most are of English origin. Count 5 for each blank correctly filled in.

Wilson's Phalarope spinning

71. LATIN ROOTS AND WORDS

Scientific names are usually composed from Greek and Latin roots. Knowledge of their meaning leads to a better understanding of the scientific names which frequently describe or allude to a characteristic feature or attribute of the species. Bird watchers, whether or not they have had Latin or Greek, frequently like to learn the meaning of these roots. Here are some of the more common ones of Latin origin found in the scientific names of North American birds.

Note: Drop the last syllable to find the root. When two forms are given (i.e., nominative and genitive), drop the last syllable of the genitive to find the root. Adjectives are given in the masculine, nominative, singular. Most are in the second declension in which the feminine ends in *a*, the neuter in *um*. Thus *aestivus, aestiva, aestivum.* Match the English with the Latin by placing the right letter in the box. Each correct answer counts 2 1/2.

Latin	English
1. Aestivus ☐	a. A bill
2. Albus ☐	b. A crest
3. Arenarius ☐	c. A foot
4. Auris ☐	d. A marsh
5. Aurum ☐	e. An ear
6. Australis ☐	f. A tail
7. Caeruleus ☐	g. Belted
8. Capillus ☐	h. -bearer
9. Cauda ☐	i. Black
10. Caurinus ☐	j. Black-capped Vireo
11. Celatus ☐	k. Black Duck
12. Cinctus ☐	l. Concealed
13. -colus ☐	m. Crowned
14. Coronatus ☐	n. Cerulean
15. Crista ☐	o. -dweller
16. Dorsum ☐	p. Gold
17. -fer ☐	q. Gray
18. Flavus ☐	r. Hair
19. Frons, frontis ☐	s. Northern

20. The range of what bird with the specific name *rubripes* is shown on the map below?

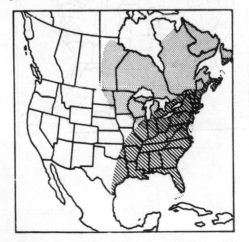

21. Griseus ☐
22. Gula ☐
23. Guttatus ☐
24. Hiemalis ☐
25. Ludovicianus ☐
26. Maculosus ☐
27. Niger ☐
28. Noveboracensis ☐
29. Nucha ☐
30. Palus, paludis ☐
31. Pes, pedis ☐
32. Pusillus ☐
33. Rostrum ☐
34. Ruber, rubra, rubrum ☐
35. Septentrionalis ☐
36. Stellatus ☐
37. Velox, velocis ☐
38. Venter, ventris ☐
39. Vireo ☐

t. Northwestern
u. Of Louisiana
v. Of New York
w. Pertaining to sands
x. Pertaining to summer
y. Pertaining to winter
z. Red
aa. Southern
bb. Spotted
cc. Spotted
dd. Starred, i.e., spotted
ee. Swift
ff. The back
gg. The belly
hh. The forehead
ii. The neck
jj. The throat
kk. To be green
ll. Very small
mm. White
nn. Yellow

40. The range of what bird with the specific name *atricapilla* is shown on the map below?

72. GREEK ROOTS AND WORDS

Scientific names are usually composed from Greek and Latin roots. Knowledge of their meaning leads to a better understanding of the scientific names, which often describe or allude to a characteristic feature or attribute of the species. Bird watchers, whether or not they have had Latin or Greek, frequently like to learn the meaning of these roots. Here are some of the more common ones of Greek origin found in the scientific names of North American birds. Match the English meanings with the Greek roots by placing the right letter in the box. Each correct answer counts 2 1/2.

Note: The letters C and K are often interchangeable. Drop the last syllable to find the root. When two forms are given they are the nominative and the genitive.

Greek	English
1. Aëtos ☐	a. A beak
2. Akantha ☐	b. A bird
3. Archos ☐	c. A chief
4. Chloros ☐	d. A claw
5. Chrysos ☐	e. A fly
6. Dendron ☐ ·	f. A foot
7. Drys, dryos ☐	g. A gnat
8. Empis, empidos ☐	h. A head
9. Erythros ☐	i. An eagle
10. Eu- ☐	j. A tail
11. Gaster ☐	k. A thorn
12. Glaukos ☐	l. A tree
13. Hesperos ☐	m. A tree
14. Hyperboreos ☐	n. A wing
15. Iris, iridos ☐	o. Arctic Loon
16. Kephale ☐	p. -bearer
17. Kerkos ☐	q. Black
18. Kyaneos ☐	r. Bluish-green
19. Leukos ☐	s. Bobolink

20. The range of what bird with the specific name *oryzivorus* is shown on the maps below?

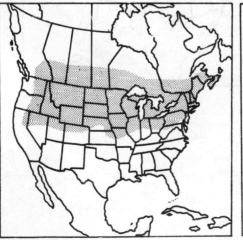

72. GREEK ROOTS AND WORDS *(Continued)*

21. Macros ☐
22. Melas, melanos ☐
23. Myia ☐
24. Notos ☐
25. Nyx, nyktos ☐
26. Onyx, onychos ☐
27. Ophthalmos ☐
28. Ornis, ornithos ☐
29. Oryza ☐
30. Ous, otos ☐
31. -phagus ☐
32. Philos ☐
33. Phone ☐
34. -phorus ☐
35. Platys ☐
36. Polios ☐
37. Pous, podos ☐
38. Pteron ☐
39. Rhynchos ☐

t. Dark blue
u. -eater
v. Flat, broad
w. Gold
x. Good, well
y. Green
z. Light gray
aa. Long, large
bb. Loving
cc. Night
dd. Of evening
ee. Of the extreme north
ff. Red
gg. Rice
hh. Sound, voice
ii. The back
jj. The belly
kk. The ear
ll. The eye
mm. The rainbow
nn. White

40. The range of what water bird with the specific name *arctica* is shown on the map below?

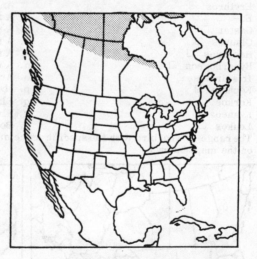

73. GENUS NAMES—SESQUIPEDALIAN

Some generic names are longer and more complicated than those in the previous genus-name quiz. All these below are names of birds that occur annually somewhere in North America. Match the English with the scientific name by placing the right letter in the box. Each correct answer counts 2 1/2.

Genus Name	English name
1. Aechmophorus ☐	a. Ancient Murrelet
2. Asyndesmus ☐	b. Ani
3. Calamospiza ☐	c. Black Swift
4. Catoptrophorus ☐	d. Black Tern
5. Chlidonias ☐	e. Cactus Wren
6. Coturnicops ☐	f. Caspian Tern
7. Crotophaga ☐	g. Cassin's Auklet
8. Gelochelidon ☐	h. Elf Owl
9. Geococcyx ☐	i. Gull-billed Tern
10. Gymnorhimus ☐	j. Ivory-billed Woodpecker
11. Heteroscelus ☐	k. Lark Bunting
12. Hydroprogne ☐	l. Least Bittern
13. Ixobrychus ☐	m. Least Petrel
14. Pedioecetes ☐	n. Lewis' Woodpecker
15. Phalaenoptilus ☐	o. Marbled Murrelet
16. Platypsaris ☐	p. McCown's Longspur
17. Plectrophenax ☐	q. Olive Sparrow
18. Rhodostethia ☐	r. Parakeet Auklet
19. Rhynchophanes ☐	s. Piñon Jay
20. Tachycineta ☐	t. Poor-will

East only

21. Arremonops ☐	u. Pygmy Owl
22. Campephilus ☐	v. Reddish Egret
23. Cistothorus ☐	w. Red-faced Warbler
24. Dichromanassa ☐	x. Roadrunner
25. Eudocimus ☐	y. Rose-throated Becard

West only

26. Brachyramphus ☐	z. Ross' Gull
27. Campylorhynchus ☐	aa. Sharp-tailed Grouse
28. Cardellina ☐	bb. Short-billed Marsh Wren
29. Cyclorrhynchus ☐	cc. Snow Bunting
30. Cypseloides ☐	dd. Spectacled Eider
31. Endomychura ☐	ee. Spotted Dove
32. Glaucidium ☐	ff. Sulphur-bellied Flycatcher
33. Halocyptena ☐	gg. Thick-billed Parrot
34. Lampronetta ☐	hh. Violet-green Swallow
35. Micrathene ☐	ii. Wandering Tattler
36. Myiodynastes ☐	jj. Western Grebe
37. Ptychoramphus ☐	kk. Willet
38. Rhynchopsitta ☐	ll. White Ibis
39. Streptopelia ☐	mm. Xantus' Murrelet
40. Synthliboramphus ☐	nn. Yellow Rail

74. HALL OF FAME

Listed below are 40 well-known ornithologists and naturalists. For each one match the description of the man or his works with his name. Each correct answer counts 2 1/2.

Name	Description

1. Allen, Joel Asaph 1838–1921 □

2. Audubon, John James 1785–1851 □

3. Bailey, Florence Merriam 1863–1948 □

4. Baird, Spencer Fullerton 1823–1887 □

5. Bartram, William 1739–1823 □

6. Bendire, Charles E. 1836–1897 □

7. Bent, Arthur C. 1866–1954 □

8. Brand, Albert R. 1889–1940 □

9. Brewster, William 1851–1919 □

10. Burroughs, John 1837–1921 □

11. Cassin, John 1813–1869 □

12. Catesby, Mark 1679–1749 □

13. Chapman, Frank M. 1864–1945 □

14. Coues, Elliot 1842–1899 □

15. Dawson, W. Leon 1873–1928 □

16. Dutcher, William 1845–1920 □

17. Dwight, Jonathan W. 1858–1929 □

18. Fisher, Albert K. 1856–1948 □

19. Forbush, Edward H. 1858–1929 □

20. Griscom, Ludlow 1890–1959 □

21. Grinnell, Joseph 1877–1939 □

a. America's foremost early naturalist and bird painter

b. Authority on Lower Rio Grande

c. Bent's predecessor

d. Bird biographer: 20 vols. *Life Histories of North American Birds* 1919–1958

e. *Birds of Massachusetts* 1925–1929

f. Famous authority on gulls

g. Canada's bird man

h. Cape May counselor

i. Chief, U.S. Biological Survey 1916–1927

j. Curator of Birds, U.S. National Museum, for 50 years

k. Earliest American naturalist

l. Early Arizona birder; U.S. Army; quail subspecies once named for him

m. Early authority on western birds

n. Early bird-photographer

o. Edited the first three *A.O.U. Check-lists.*

p. Father of life zones

q. First in the field (20th cent.)

r. First woman Fellow of the A.O.U.; *Birds of New Mexico*, 1928

s. Founder of the National Association of Audubon Societies

t. *Handbook of Birds of Eastern North America*, 1895

u. *Hawks and Owls of the United States in Their Relation to Agriculture*

22. Harris, Edward 1799-1863☐
23. Henshaw, Henry W. 1850-1930 ☐
24. Job, Herbert K. 1864-1933 ☐
25. Lincoln, Frederick 1892-1961 ☐
26. Mearns, Edgar A. 1856-1916 ☐
27. Merriam, C. Hart 1855-1942 ☐
28. Nelson, Edward W. 1854-1934 ☐
29. Nuttall, Thomas 1786-1859 ☐
30. Reed, Chester A. 1876-1912 ☐
31. Ridgway, Robert 1850-1929 ☐
32. Sennett, George B. 1840-1900 ☐
33. Steller, George W. 1709-1746 ☐
34. Stone, Witmer 1866-1939 ☐
35. Taverner, Percy A. 1875-1947 ☐
36. Thayer, John Eliot 1862-1933 ☐
37. Van Tyne, Josselyn 1902-1956 ☐
38. Wayne, Arthur T. 1863-1930 ☐
39. Wilson, Alexander 1766-1813 ☐

v. He found Florida beautiful
w. His realm: the Carolina Low Country
x. *Key to North American Birds*, 1872
y. Mentor from Michigan
z. Monitor of migration
aa. Naturalist with Vitus Bering
bb. Nestor of the MVZ
cc. Omniscient in oölogy
dd. Oölogist; *Birds of California*, 1923
ee. Oracle of October Farm
ff. Pioneer American ornithologist and botanist; bird club named for him
gg. Pioneer recorder of birds' songs
hh. Preceded Audubon; *American Ornithology*, 1810
ii. *Land Birds* for the hip pocket
jj. Sage of "Slabsides"
kk. Secretary of Smithsonian, 1878-1887; co-author *A History of North American Birds*, 1874-1884
ll. Sometime chief, U.S. Biological Survey
mm. Went up the Missouri with Audubon

40. The range of what buteo hawk named after William_____(1789-1855), an English ornithologist, is shown on the maps below?

 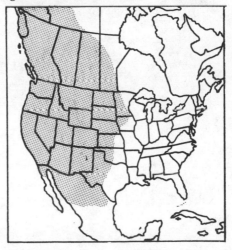

ANSWERS

ROCK DOVE

MOURNING DOVE

ROCK DOVE

ANSWERS

Quiz 1

1. j.	5. t.	9. k.	13. m	17. b.
2. r.	6. g.	10. s.	14. c	18. e.
3. o.	7. p.	11. h.	15. a.	19. d.
4. l.	8. i.	12. f.	16. n.	20. q.

Quiz 2

1. Brant, Duck, Hawk, Oyster-catcher, Petrel, Phoebe, Rail, Rosy Finch, Swift, Tern, Turnstone, Vulture
2. Goose, Grosbeak, Grouse, Jay
3. Gnatcatcher
4. Booby, Creeper, Pelican, Thrasher, Towhee
5. Teal
6. Gull
7. Eagle, Plover
8. Flycatcher, Hawk, Jay
9. Heron
10. Owl
11. Heron
12. Heron, Jay, Kingfisher
13. Bunting
14. Gull
15. Bunting
16. Finch, Gallinule, Martin, Sandpiper
17. Crossbill, Phalarope
18. Duck, Turnstone
19. Blackbird
20. Tanager
21. Bunting, Goose
22. Egret, Owl, Plover
23. Shearwater, Tern
24. Ibis, Pelican, Wagtail
25. Rail, Wagtail, Warbler

Quiz 3

1. Woodpecker
2. Grebe
3. Flicker
4. Hawk
5. Hawk
6. Blackbird
7. Nuthatch
8. Pigeon, Sparrow
9. Vireo
10. Dove, Goose
11. Hawk, Kite, Ptarmigan, Tropic-bird
12. Sparrow, Swift
13. Dove, Crossbill, Junco, Scoter
14. Warbler
15. Gull (Great), Three-toed Woodpecker
16. Plover, Tree Duck
17. Cuckoo, Magpie
18. Chickadee, Petrel, Vireo
19. Night Heron
20. Grosbeak, Gull, Oriole
21. Stilt
22. Warbler
23. Warbler
24. Warbler
25. Warbler

Quiz 4

1. Swallow
2. Owl, Swallow
3. Waxwing
4. Swallow
5. Finch, Sparrow, Wren
6. Hawk, Wren (Long-billed, Short-billed)
7. Bluebird, Chickadee
8. Warbler

9. Dove, Ptarmigan, Sandpiper, Wren
10. Grouse, Sparrow, Thrasher
11. Crane
12. Sparrow
13. Bunting, Goose
14. Grouse
15. Scoter
16. Sparrow, Duck (Black-bellied, Fulvous)
17. Plover
18. Pipit
19. Duck, Ibis, Thrush
20. Sparrow
21. Warbler
22. Oriole
23. Warbler
24. Grosbeak, Siskin, Warbler
25. Chicken (Greater, Lesser), Falcon, Warbler

Quiz 5

1. Ruby-throated or Anna's Hummingbird, 3 1/2 in.; Downy Woodpecker, 6 in.; Robin, 10 in.; Yellow-billed Cuckoo, 12 in.; Rock Dove, 15 in.; Common Crow, 20 in.
2. Boat-tailed Grackle, 16 in.; Blue or Steller's Jay, 12 in.; Great Crested Flycatcher, 9 in.; Horned Lark, 7 in.; Tree Swallow, 6 in.; House Wren, 5 in.
3. Ovenbird, House Sparrow, Tufted Titmouse, Red-eyed Vireo—all 5 1/2 to 6 in.
4. A, about 5 in.: American Redstart, Chipping Sparrow, Yellow Warbler
   B, about 8 in.: Brown-headed Cowbird, Baltimore or Bullock's Oriole, Starling
   C, about 10 in.: Sparrow Hawk, Killdeer, Whip-poor-will
5. Mourning Dove, Red-shafted or Yellow-shafted Flicker, Belted Kingfisher, Brown Thrasher—all about 12 in.
6. Bald Eagle, Herring Gull, Turkey Vulture—all scavengers
7. Blue-gray Gnatcatcher, Veery, Red-eyed Vireo—all insect eaters
8. Bobwhite, American Goldfinch, White-throated Sparrow—all seed eaters
9. Peregrine Falcon, Cooper's Hawk, Screech Owl—all meat-eaters
10. Great Blue Heron, Belted Kingfisher, Common Tern—all fish-eaters

Quiz 6

1. f.	5. r.	9. l.	13. k.	17. b.
2. a.	6. h.	10. j.	14. c.	18. t.
3. e.	7. i.	11. n.	15. p.	19. s.
4. g.	8. o.	12. m.	16. q.	20. d.

Quiz 7

1. i.	5. m.	9. c.	13. h.	17. l.
2. n.	6. e.	10. j.	14. o.	18. s.
3. k.	7. d.	11. g.	15. f.	19. q.
4. p.	8. a.	12. r.	16. t.	20. b.

Quiz 8

1. l.	5. a.	9. n.	13. j.	17. i.
2. t.	6. g.	10. f.	14. m.	18. q.
3. e.	7. k.	11. p.	15. s.	19. r.
4. d.	8. o.	12. h.	16. b.	20. c.

Quiz 9

1. c.	5. d.	9. a.	13. f.	17. s.
2. k.	6. o.	10. h.	14. j.	18. r.
3. t.	7. e.	11. p.	15. i.	19. g.
4. b.	8. m.	12. n.	16. l.	20. q.

Quiz 10

1. k.	5. l.	9. a.	13. r.	17. o.
2. s.	6. b.	10. j.	14. h.	18. e.
3. m.	7. c.	11. d.	15. i.	19. q.
4. p.	8. f.	12. t.	16. g.	20. n.

Quiz 11

1. Black Duck
2. Starling
3. Robin
4. Crow
5. Turkey Vulture
6. Great Blue Heron
7. Canada Goose
8. Common Egret
9. Nighthawk
10. Barn Swallow
11. Flicker
12. Sparrow Hawk
13. Purple Martin
14. Grackle
15. Goldfinch
16. Black Vulture
17. Swift
18. Bald Eagle
19. Herring Gull
20. Blue or Steller's Jay

Quiz 12

1. i.	5. p.	9. k.	13. m.	17. a.
2. n.	6. s.	10. l.	14. c.	18. g.
3. f.	7. o.	11. q.	15. r.	19. h.
4. d.	8. e.	12. b.	16. j.	20. t.

Quiz 13

1. B.	5. B.	9. B.	13. A.	17. A, B.
2. B.	6. C.	10. E.	14. A.	18. D.
3. A.	7. D.	11. E.	15. C.	19. C.
4. A, B.	8. C.	12. E.	16. A.	20. D.

Quiz 14

1. Argentina
2. Shorebirds
3. Neither. Each forms a link in the chain of life. Predators keep a stock healthy by taking the sick, crippled, and aged
4. Loss of habitat
5. Ivory-billed Woodpecker
6. Heath Hen
7. 442
8. Passenger Pigeon
9. Eskimo Curlew
10. Rodents
11. Upland Plover
12. Excessive commercial exploitation
13. Excessive use of powerful pesticides
14. Slaughter of egrets
15. California Condor
16. 8,000,000
17. Hawk Mountain Sanctuary, Kempton, Pa.
18. Bird hawks
19. Wetlands
20. Barrier beaches

Quiz 15

1. t.	5. k.	9. j.	13. l.	17. e.
2. p.	6. f.	10. d.	14. i.	18. c.
3. b.	7. r.	11. a.	15. h.	19. q.
4. o.	8. g.	12. m.	16. n.	20. s.

Quiz 16

1. b.	5. p.	9. f.	13. q.	17. k.
2. o.	6. e.	10. i.	14. t.	18. c.
3. a.	7. g.	11. l.	15. m.	19. h.
4. d.	8. j.	12. n.	16. r.	20. s.

Quiz 17

1. Flycatcher, Sandpiper
2. Longspur
3. Kinglet, Sparrow
4. Woodpecker
5. Thrush
6. Teal
7. Towhee
8. Warbler; Thrush (former name of a subspecies of Swainson's)
9. Flycatcher
10. Warbler
11. Kinglet
12. Sparrow
13. Junco
14. Scoter
15. Cuckoo, Loon, Magpie
16. Chat
17. Blackbird
18. Flicker
19. Warbler
20. Warbler
21. Cowbird, Nuthatch
22. Hummingbird
23. Warbler
24. Warbler
25. Warbler
26. Woodpecker
27. Grosbeak
28. Becard
29. Hummingbird
30. Vireo, Warbler
31. Flycatcher
32. Hummingbird
33. Chickadee
34. Trogon
35. Gull
36. Chickadee, Junco
37. Shearwater
38. Sandpiper
39. Sparrow
40. Flycatcher

Quiz 18

1. Kingfisher
2. Oriole, Merganser, Warbler
3. Woodpecker
4. Godwit, Murrelet
5. Sandpiper
6. Grebe
7. Gull
8. Duck, Pheasant
9. Plover, Turtle Dove
10. Petrel, Quail
11. Hawk
12. Owl
13. Duck
14. Oriole
15. Pigeon
16. Godwit
17. Tern, Titmouse
18. Titmouse
19. Eider
20. Dove, Owl
21. Hummingbird
22. Thrasher
23. Tern
24. Curlew, Dowitcher, Marsh Wren, Thrasher
25. Owl
26. Jaeger
27. Hawk
28. Swallow
29. Flycatcher

30. Hawk
31. Grouse, Sandpiper, Sparrow
32. Owl
33. Hawk
34. Dowitcher, Marsh Wren
35. Hawk
36. Kite
37. Hummingbird
38. Curlew
39. Shearwater
40. Murre, Parrot

Quiz 19

1. Avocet, Bittern, Coot, Flamingo, Goldfinch, Golden Plover, Oystercatcher, Redstart, Widgeon, Woodcock
2. Loon, Tern, Warbler
3. Waxwing
4. Goose, Warbler
5. Tern
6. Goldfinch, Tree Sparrow, Widgeon
7. Longspur
8. Shearwater
9. Warbler
10. Junco
11. Warbler
12. Rail
13. Flycatcher
14. Duck,* Swallow,* Honeycreeper*
15. Oriole
16. Petrel
17. Warbler
   *—Accidental
   **—Extinct

18. Sparrow
19. Chickadee, Parakeet,** Wren
20. Warbler
21. Warbler
22. Golden Plover
23. Godwit
24. Gull
25. Sparrow
26. Warbler
27. Duck**
28. Heron
29. Kite
30. Vireo
31. Petrel*
32. Tree Duck*
33. Tern
34. Jay, Woodpecker
35. Condor, Gull, Quail, Thrasher
36. Woodpecker
37. Caracara,** Junco, Petrel**
38. Albatross
39. Chickadee, Duck, Jay, Junco
40. Shearwater

Quiz 20

1. q.	5. e.	9. k.	13. n.	17. g.
2. b.	6. i.	10. p.	14. d.	18. t.
3. l.	7. h.	11. r.	15. o.	19. c.
4. j.	8. f.	12. m.	16. s.	20. a.

Quiz 21

1. A boatman on the Missouri River; the species migrates along river valleys
2. A sewer outlet
3. A fresh-water marsh at dawn
4. Possible (flying over the ocean, often diving)
5. A Snowy Egret
6. Salt or brackish marshes
7. Whichever is nearer
8. Salt
9. Fresh
10. No
11. At sea or on a rock jetty; it likes rocks not sand
12. Fresh-water marsh
13. Whichever is nearer
14. Black-crowned
15. The grassy edges of a fresh-water marsh and a short-grass salt marsh

16. Marshes, fresh-water or salt
17. Cattle
18. Green
19. Pelagic
20. Unlikely (but not impossible)

Quiz 22

1. Red-breasted; the Common is more common on fresh water
2. Never; it occurs on fresh water only
3. A bay
4. Fresh-water ponds
5. Ring-necked Ducks; Canvasbacks are birds of prairie sloughs in summer, bays or estuaries in winter
6. Not
7. Shallow water
8. Greater Scaup; Gadwall would not have liked the salt water of Boston Harbor
9. True
10. Near shore, over the shoals, where they dive for shellfish
11. Sometimes
12. Winter; it summers on the tundra
13. Greater; Lessers are more often found on fresh water
14. It can be found in such a variety of places
15. The ocean
16. Will
17. No, probably neither; Shovelers are fresh-water ducks; October, when he sailed back, is too early for Oldsquaws
18. Yes
19. Hooded Mergansers; Ruddies breed in open marshes
20. Pilgrims; Harlequins like "a stern and rock-bound coast," not a sandy coast as that of Virginia

Quiz 23

1. Surfbird; Western Sandpiper likes sandy beaches
2. In the salt marshes
3. Yes; and by any other shoreline of fresh and (sometimes) salt water
4. Ruddy Turnstone
5. The prairies
6. Least
7. Semipalmated
8. Marshes
9. Deserts and plains
10. Grassy marshes
11. Wet
12. Shallow pools
13. Airfields and open cemeteries
14. Killdeer; they are commonly seen on golf courses
15. American Oystercatcher; Purple Sandpiper likes rocks
16. Swamps
17. Fields
18. Dry
19. No. Clams live in sand and mud. Black Turnstones like rocky coasts.

20. No. Clams live in sand and mud. Black Oystercatchers like rocky coasts.

Quiz 24

1. On the ground in a circle facing out
2. In large flocks
3. A long
4. Buff-breasted Sandpiper; Yellowlegs are too noisy
5. Hudsonian Godwit; Stilts are too noisy
6. A goose; geese walk better than ducks
7. Red; Wilson's spins more
8. True
9. Wandering Tattler
10. Spruce Grouse
11. Horned Grebes
12. Chairman of the Board; it has a sedate, dignified appearance
13. Elaborate
14. Killdeer
15. In trees
16. In groups of a dozen or more
17. Does
18. American Woodcock
19. American Oystercatcher
20. Long-billed Curlew

Quiz 25

1. No; it roosts in groups of several dozen to 100 or more
2. Great Horned Owl
3. Lower
4. Showy Owl
5. Yellow-throated Vireo
6. Gray
7. Boreal
8. False; just the opposite is true
9. Rock Wren
10. False; the owl may grab at his hat
11. Usually
12. Bald
13. Less
14. Eastern or Western Bluebird
15. Cedar Waxwing; pairs appear affectionate; on the other hand, male House Wrens are often polygamous
16. Water Pipit
17. Water Pipit
18. Long-billed Marsh Wren
19. Winter Wren
20. Evening Grosbeak; the Cedar Waxwing occasionally gets drunk on overripe berries

Quiz 26

1. Crepuscular
2. Gray-crowned Rosy Finch
3. Lark
4. Pine Grosbeak
5. Low
6. Cassin's
7. Rose-breasted
8. Dawn and dusk
9. Lord
10. Red Crossbill
11. Rufous-sided Towhee
12. Crossbills, Redpolls, Siskins
13. Slate-colored Junco; it likes to bathe in dry snow
14. Tree; they often sing in chorus
15. Indigo
16. Horned Larks, Longspurs, Snow Buntings
17. Seaside
18. Dickcissel (a bird of the roadside wire; Le Conte's is too secretive)
19. Brown
20. Black-headed

Quiz 27

1. No
2. Yes; it seeks safety just by squatting on the ground where its brown-striped plumage often blends with the surroundings
3. Less; the Lesser is the more gregarious
4. Pied-billed Grebe
5. Common Gallinule, Purple Gallinule, Jacana
6. False; it nests in trees
7. Seldom
8. Sometimes
9. Dowitcher (both species)
10. Stilt Sandpiper
11. Lesser Yellowlegs and Solitary Sandpiper
12. Red-throated
13. Western
14. Mugwump; it is often a fence sitter, or fence-post percher, "mug" on one side, "wump" on the other
15. Senator
16. Anhinga
17. Cattle Egret
18. Snowy Egret
19. Louisiana Heron
20. Reddish Egret

Quiz 28

1. Yes
2. Yes; but after nesting and through the winter they roost in coveys of four or five dozen birds
3. Teeter
4. Both
5. Both
6. In running away
7. Chukar Partridges
8. All
9. False; they usually roost in the snow
10. In running
11. High
12. Under
13. Both feet at once
14. 18 m.p.h.
15. Often
16. Low
17. Often
18. Scrub
19. Scaled
20. Brewer's (Redwinged does not)

Quiz 29

1. Walks
2. Walks
3. Hops
4. Both
5. Walks
6. Hops
7. Hops
8. Walks
9. Both
10. Hops (runs, too)
11. Walks
12. Hops
13. Both
14. Walks
15. Hops
16. Hops
17. Hops
18. Both (runs, too)
19. Walks
20. Walks

Quiz 30

1. Gadwall
2. American Widgeon
3. Canvasback (up to 72 m.p.h.)
4. White-fronted Geese; Brant fly in irregular flocks, undulating
5. Common Eiders
6. Abreast
7. Oldsquaw
8. Male
9. Mute
10. Canvasback

11. High
12. Common
13. In V-shaped wedges, with necks extended
14. Ruddy
15. True
16. Do both
17. Low
18. Loose V's
19. Common Goldeneye; also Steller's Eider, Green-winged Teal
20. Gadwall

Quiz 31

1. Slower
2. Yes
3. Diving
4. Yellow-crowned Night Heron
5. White
6. Green Heron
7. Least Bittern
8. American Bittern
9. Common Loon, Red-necked Grebe
10. Common
11. Black-crowned Night Heron
12. Red-throated
13. Common
14. Leach's
15. Wilson's
16. Great
17. Fulmar
18. Wilson's, (Leach's is not)
19. Audubon's
20. True

Quiz 32

1. h.	5. l.	9. e.	13. n.	17. False
2. j.	6. i.	10. d.	14. g.	18. True
3. k.	7. c.	11. m.	15. True	19. False
4. f.	8. a.	12. b.	16. True	20. Osprey

Quiz 33

1. Northern Shrike
2. Long
3. Mountain
4. Dipper
5. Red-breasted
6. Townsend's Solitaire
7. Wheatear
8. Starling
9. Blue-gray Gnatcatcher
10. Buoyant, erratic, undulating
11. Gray-cheeked, Swainson's
12. Yellow-breasted Chat
13. Common Grackle
14. Long-billed
15. Philadelphia
16. Connecticut Warbler; the Redstart is our most active warbler
17. Prothonotary Warbler, Northern Waterthrush
18. Common Bushtit
19. Hutton's
20. Phainopepla

Quiz 34

1. e.	5. b.	9. d.	13. p.	17. n.
2. g.	6. i.	10. a.	14. l.	18. s.
3. h.	7. c.	11. k.	15. o.	19. q.
4. f.	8. j.	12. r.	16. t.	20. m.

Quiz 35

1. h.	5. c.	9. a.	13. r.	17. t.
2. n.	6. q.	10. m.	14. e.	18. p.
3. o.	7. f.	11. l.	15. g.	19. d.
4. b.	8. i.	12. s.	16. k.	20. j.

Quiz 36

1. p.	5. s.	9. t.	13. a.	17. b.
2. c.	6. h.	10. o.	14. d.	18. e.
3. r.	7. n.	11. j.	15. i.	19. l.
4. q.	8. g.	12. f.	16. m.	20. k.

Quiz 37

1. Black-crowned
2. Lesser
3. Black-bellied; the Golden flies to South America over the Atlantic
4. Sanderling
5. Caspian
6. Bald
7. Pied-billed
8. Turkey
9. Franklin's
10. Greater
11. White-winged
12. Willow; too far south for the Rock
13. Did not; too far south
14. Double-cresteds; Greats would not be that far south on that date
15. Glossy
16. Broad-winged or Swainson's
17. Common Egrets
18. White-faced
19. Greater
20. California

Quiz 38

1. a.	5. p.	9. j.	13. s.	17. h.
2. t.	6. i.	10. m.	14. o.	18. e.
3. c.	7. g.	11. q.	15. k.	19. f.
4. n.	8. r.	12. b.	16. d.	20. l.

Quiz 39

1. Saw-whet
2. Goshawk; Harris' is an open country species of the Southwest
3. Ferruginous
4. Great Horned Owls
5. Barn Owl, which likes the structures of man; the Great Horned Owl does not
6. Long-eared
7. Red-shouldered; Red-tailed likes drier woods
8. Wood edges
9. Near water
10. The mountains
11. False; they will accept smaller tracts than the Red-tailed
12. Barred Owl
13. False; open spaces are just what it likes
14. Great Gray Owl
15. Short-tailed Hawk
16. Broad-winged
17. Spotted, which likes canyons more than does the Elf. He lived, you remember "in a cavern, in a canyon, excavating for a mine".
18. Boreal
19. Elf
20. Canyons

Quiz 40

1. Ivory
2. Little
3. Herring
4. Ross'; it is thought to winter in the Arctic Ocean
5. Bonaparte's; it nests in conifers
6. California
7. Franklin's
8. Laughing

9. Black-headed
10. Glaucous
11. Lower
12. Black
13. Coastal islands and marshes
14. Caspian
15. Sandy coastal islands and marshes
16. Least
17. Outer islands
18. Sandwich
19. Arctic
20. Sooty

Quiz 41

1. Downy or Ladder-backed which frequents houses and feeders; Hairy prefers woods
2. Lewis'; Pileated likes deep woods
3. False, the loblollies should be over 70 years old and suffering from red-heart disease
4. Black-backed Three-toed; Golden-fronted is a bird of dry, open country of the Southwest
5. An apple grower; Red-headeds prefer orchards to deep woods
6. b.
7. d.
8. c.
9. i.
10. h.
11. g.
12. e.
13. a.
14. f.
15. l.
16. k.
17. o.
18. j.
19. m.
20. n.

Quiz 42

1. Hooded
2. Whistling
3. Ross'
4. Yes
5. By lying close
6. True; it makes twice as many
7. Ruddy Turnstone
8. Northern
9. In the snow
10. Uphill
11. Up into trees
12. Elaborate courtship
13. A dance hall; they have a strutting nuptial performance, but no song
14. 100
15. Yes
16. Marsh
17. Short-eared
18. Shrike
19. Often
20. Sluggish

Quiz 43

1. Near the ground
2. False; the Solitary moves about more as it sings
3. True
4. Black-throated Blue or Black-throated Gray Warbler
5. Swainson's
6. Olive-backed
7. Wag their tails
8. Yellow Warblers
9. Kentucky
10. Cape May
11. Treetops
12. Feign a broken wing
13. From the ground to the treetops
14. Hooded (Wilson's has neither the habit nor the white tips)
15. Palm Warblers
16. Prothonotary
17. High
18. Creep along the trunk or branches
19. Worm-eating Warblers or Waterthrushes
20. Lucy's

Quiz 44

1. Burrowing, Short-eared, Snowy
2. True
3. Pompous orator
4. Hawk Owl
5. Near trunk, high up
6. Lewis' Woodpecker, Red-shafted and Yellow-shafted Flickers
7. Yellow-bellied Sapsucker
8. Red-cockaded
9. True
10. True
11. False; it does twitch its tail
12. Kiskadee Flycatcher
13. True
14. Occasionally
15. f.
16. e.
17. b. or c.
18. d.
19. c.
20. a.

Quiz 45

1. True
2. Tilter
3. True
4. With back level
5. True
6. True
7. True
8. "Stern high"
9. Kittiwake
10. Swim and dive
11. False; it can
12. False; it swims with neck drawn in
13. b.
14. c.
15. f.
16. e.
17. d.
18. a.
19. h.
20. g.

Quiz 46

1. True
2. True
3. Long-billed
4. True
5. False
6. Red
7. Wilson's
8. Rocket
9. No; the Common Snipe takes off in swift zigzags
10. Whimbrel
11. Pectoral
12. Spotted
13. Buff-breasted
14. Sanderling
15. All except American Wood-cock
16. True
17. Mountain Plover; the wingpits of the American Golden Plover are gray
18. Hudsonian
19. Purple Sandpiper
20. Black Turnstone

Quiz 47

1. c.
2. g.
3. d.
4. b.
5. k.
6. a.
7. h.
8. f.
9. e.
10. j.
11. i.
12. m.
13. p.
14. l.
15. o.
16. t.
17. n.
18. s.
19. r.
20. q.

Quiz 48

1. d.	5. i.	9. b.	13. o.	17. s.
2. a.	6. j.	10. c.	14. l.	18. q.
3. f.	7. e.	11. h.	15. n.	19. r.
4. g.	8. k.	12. m.	16. p.	20. t.

Quiz 49

1. Bank
2. Rough-winged
3. Violet-green
4. True
5. False; the opposite is true
6. True
7. Yes
8. Undulating
9. False; wingbeat of the Steller's is slower
10. Clark's Nutcracker
11. Fish Crow
12. False
13. Common Raven
14. Common Raven
15. True
16. True
17. Mexican
18. Piñon
19. Mexican
20. Gray

Quiz 50

1. c.	5. e.	9. q.	13. j.	17. f.
2. g.	6. t.	10. d.	14. b.	18. l.
3. p.	7. k.	11. a.	15. s.	19. m.
4. n.	8. o.	12. h.	16. i.	20. r.

Quiz 51

1. d.	5. s.	9. a.	13. c.	17. o.
2. h.	6. p.	10. n.	14. e.	18. l.
3. k.	7. i.	11. g.	15. j.	19. r.
4. t.	8. q.	12. m.	16. b.	20. f.

Quiz 52

1. b.	5. e.	9. a.	13. p.	17. t.
2. h.	6. d.	10. j.	14. k.	18. l.
3. c.	7. f.	11. r.	15. m.	19. q.
4. g.	8. i.	12. s.	16. o.	20. Chimney Swift

Quiz 53

1. a.	5. f.	9. g.	13. q.	17. m.
2. d.	6. b.	10. k.	14. t.	18. l.
3. e.	7. j.	11. h.	15. s.	19. p.
4. c.	8. i.	12. o.	16. r.	20. n.

Quiz 54

1. White-necked Raven
2. Common Raven
3. Yellow-billed
4. Solitary
5. Ruby-throated
6. Eastern
7. Probably saw both species; their ranges overlap in Montana

8. Chimney
9. Hermit
10. Eastern
11. Chestnut-collared
12. Green
13. Carolina

14. Steller's
15. Tree
16. Black-capped
17. Acadian Flycatcher
18. Rough-winged
19. Yellow-bellied Flycatcher
20. Cedar

Quiz 55

1. jj.	9. r.	17. dd.	25. u.	33. d.
2. y.	10. l.	18. i.	26. aa.	34. f.
3. h.	11. ff.	19. v.	27. z.	35. k.
4. nn.	12. x.	20. p.	28. bb.	36. ii.
5. j.	13. m.	21. w.	29. kk.	37. q.
6. b.	14. t.	22. e.	30. hh.	38. c.
7. s.	15. cc.	23. n.	31. o.	39. mm.
8. a.	16. ll.	24. g.	32. gg.	40. ee.

Quiz 56

1. nn.	9. l.	17. f.	25. e.	33. jj.
2. s.	10. cc.	18. g.	26. o.	34. c.
3. a.	11. hh.	19. p.	27. y.	35. ii.
4. mm.	12. t.	20. m.	28. bb.	36. dd.
5. j.	13. ee.	21. u.	29. r.	37. b.
6. k.	14. h.	22. v.	30. aa.	38. w.
7. q.	15. n.	23. ll.	31. x.	39. kk.
8. d.	16. i.	24. gg.	32. z.	40. ff.

Quiz 57

1. Booby
2. Swallow
3. Dipper
4. Thrush
5. Loon, Cuckoo
6. Bunting
7. Redhead
8. Condor
9. Kite
10. Skimmer

11. Nutcracker
12. Goose
13. Falcon
14. Crane
15. Gull
16. Cardinal
17. Rail
18. Tattler
19. Eagle
20. Crow

Quiz 58

1. Shearwater
2. Duck
3. Grouse
4. Rook*
5. Gull
6. Crane
7. Lark
8. Quail
9. Hawk

*European

10. Killdeer
11. Parrot
12. Ruff
13. Crow
14. Rail
15. Kite
16. Flicker
17. Snipe
18. Swallow
19. Chat
20. Knot

Quiz 59

1. Dove	9. Pelican, owl
2. Quails	10. Eagle
3. Partridge	11. Turtle (dove)
4. Peacocks	12. Stork, crane
5. Ravens	13. Doves
6. Ostrich	14. Sparrows
7. Hawk	15. Hen, chickens
8. Sparrow, swallow	16. Cock

Quiz 60

1. f.	5. p.	9. q.	13. b.	17. k.
2. m.	6. c.	10. o.	14. e.	18. a.
3. h.	7. g.	11. i.	15. n.	19. s.
4. t.	8. j.	12. l.	16. d.	20. r.

Quiz 61

1. q.	5. t.	9. m.	13. d.	17. b.
2. o.	6. i.	10. c.	14. p.	18. a.
3. e.	7. s.	11. g.	15. n.	19. h.
4. j.	8. f.	12. k.	16: r.	20. l.

Quiz 62

1. f.	5. m.	9. n.	13. g.	17. p.
2. i.	6. e.	10. o.	14. r.	18. c.
3. h.	7. b.	11. k.	15. a.	19. s.
4. q.	8. l.	12. j.	16. t.	20. d.

Quiz 63

1. Ani	14. Smew	28. Tanager
2. Caracara	15. Moa	29. Ern
3. Oriole	16. Bubo.	30. Tern
4. Gier	17. Jaeger	31. Fink
5. Arara	18. Asio	32. Junco
6. Shrike	19. Ara	33. Ajaia
7. Serin	20. Petrel	34. Auk
8. Sora	21. Pato	35. Olor
9. Rallus	22. Ibis	36. Eagle
10. Columba	23. Rhea	37. Anhinga
11. Eider	24. Raven	38. Anser
12. Bald	25. Drongo	39. Poult
13. Glede	26. Crow	40. Emu
	27. Roc	

Quiz 64

1. Marabou	6. Pukeko	11. Chink
2. Kori	7. Kahu	12. Crex
3. Kiwi	8. Hornero	13. Grus
4. Mynah	9. Otis	14. Rotche
5. Trogon	10. Buteo	15. Kaka

16. Anas	24. Dodo	33. Aythya
17. Roa-roa	25. Tyto	34. Xema
18. Scaup	26. Brolga	35. Kea
19. Shama	27. Oi	36. Bittern
20. Corella	28. Weka	37. Jacamar
21. Avocet	29. Ortolan	38. Ouzel
22. Rouen	30. Koel	39. Tody
23. Huia	31. Bulbul	40. Aix
	32. Egret	

Quiz 65

1. Kakapo	14. Gavia	28. Akepa
2. Rosella	15. Menura	29. Pape
3. Jabiru	16. Pie	30. Tui
4. Mopoke	17. Pica	31. Seapie
5. Oo	18. Gnow	32. Galah
6. Palila	19. Argala	33. Mamo
7. Larus	20. Maleo	34. Lulu
8. Ou	21. Sitta	35. Seesee
9. Nene	22. Mimus	36. Apapane
10. Pern	23. Coly	37. Mew
11. Colibri	24. Kagu	38. Iiwi
12. Tesa	25. Noio	39. Jacana
13. Shikra	26. Ratite	40. Prion
	27. Takahe	

Quiz 66

1. gg.	9. y.	17. p.	25. kk.	33. d.
2. hh.	10. h.	18. u.	26. ee.	34. t.
3. bb.	11. aa.	19. j.	27. nn.	35. a.
4. i.	12. k.	20. e.	28. ii.	36. n.
5. g.	13. mm.	21. f.	29. r.	37. w.
6. cc.	14. v.	22. x.	30. ff.	38. l.
7. q.	15. z.	23. m.	31. b.	39. o.
8. c.	16. jj.	24. dd.	32. s.	40. ll.

Quiz 67

1. Traill's Flycatcher
2. Northern Three-toed Woodpecker
3. Black-backed Three-toed
   Woodpecker
4. Western Kingbird
5. Thick-billed Murre
6. Sandwich Tern
7. Kiskadee Flycatcher
8. Peregrine Falcon
9. Common Teal
10. Common Gallinule
11. Red-necked Grebe
12. Whimbrel
13. Gray Partridge
14. Swainson's Thrush
15. Dunlin
16. Boreal Owl
17. Lesser Nighthawk
18. Olive Sparrow
19. Common Snipe
20. Dusky Flycatcher

Quiz 68

1. Harlequin Quail
2. Boreal Chickadee
3. Black-headed Oriole
4. Gray-cheeked Thrush
5. Common Grackle
6. Leach's Petrel
7. Sage Sparrow
8. Snowy Egret
9. Canada Goose
10. Nashville Warbler
11. Scrub Jay
12. Western Bluebird
13. Common Bushtit
14. Orange-crowned Warbler
15. Williamson's Sapsucker
16. Peregrine Falcon
17. Wilson's Warbler
18. Black-tailed Gnatcatcher
19. Rufous-sided Towhee
20. Great Blue Heron

Quiz 69

1. j.	5. d.	9. b.	13. n.	17. p.
2. s.	6. e.	10. f.	14. r.	18. l.
3. t.	7. k.	11. h.	15. o.	19. m.
4. c.	8. a.	12. g.	16. q.	20. i.

Quiz 70

1. Quail
2. Goldfinches
3. Widgeon
4. Rooks
5. Coots
6. Partridge
7. Sheldrakes
8. Larks
9. Woodcocks
10. Geese
11. Peacocks
12. Pheasants
13. Ducks
14. Herons
15. Mallards
16. Teal
17. Plovers
18. Nightingales
19. Swan
20. Snipe

Quiz 71

1. x.	9. f.	17. h.	25. u.	33. a.
2. mm.	10. t.	18. nn.	26. cc.	34. z.
3. w.	11. l.	19. hh.	27. i.	35. s.
4. e.	12. g.	20. k.	28. v.	36. dd.
5. p.	13. o.	21. q.	29. ii.	37. ee.
6. aa.	14. m.	22. jj.	30. d.	38. gg.
7. n.	15. b.	23. bb.	31. c.	39. kk.
8. r.	16. ff.	24. y.	32. ll.	40. j.

Quiz 72

1. l.	9. ff.	17. j.	25. cc.	33. hh.
2. k.	10. x.	18. t.	26. d.	34. p.
3. c.	11. jj.	19. nn.	27. ll.	35. v.
4. y.	12. z.	20. s.	28. b.	36. z.
5. w.	13. dd.	21. aa.	29. gg.	37. f.
6. ll.	14. ee.	22. g.	30. kk.	38. n.
7. m.	15. mm.	23. e.	31. u.	39. a.
8. g.	16. h.	24. ii.	32. bb.	40. o.

Quiz 73

1. jj.	9. x.	17. cc.	25. ll.	33. m.
2. n.	10. s.	18. z.	26. o.	34. dd.
3. k.	11. ii.	19. p.	27. e.	35. h.
4. kk.	12. f.	20. hh.	28. w.	36. ff.
5. d.	13. l.	21. q.	29. r.	37. g.
6. nn.	14. aa.	22. j.	30. c.	38. gg.
7. b.	15. t.	23. bb.	31. mm.	39. ee.
8. i.	16. y.	24. v.	32. u.	40. a.

Quiz 74

1. o.	9. ee.	17. f.	25. z.	33. aa.
2. a.	10. jj.	18. u.	26. l.	34. h.
3. r.	11. m.	19. e.	27. p.	35. g.
4. kk.	12. k.	20. q.	28. i.	36. cc.
5. v.	13. t.	21. bb.	29. ff.	37. y.
6. c.	14. x.	22. mm.	30. ii.	38. w.
7. d.	15. dd.	23. ll.	31. j.	39. hh.
8. gg.	16. s.	24. n.	32. b.	40. Swainson